D1304160

My Fun with Learning

4

Real-Life Heroes

·

America's Story

The Southwestern Company

Nashville, Tennessee

PRINTED ON RECYCLED PAPER

ABOUT THE AUTHORS

Raymond V. Hand, Jr., is a writer and editor specializing in reference and other nonfiction books. He is joint author with Eugene Ehrlich of *The NBC Handbook of Pronunciation.* Among the books to which he has contributed are *The Oxford Illustrated Literary Guide to the United States, The Macmillan Concise Dictionary of World History,* and *The Harper Book of American Quotations.*

For 40 years *Jack B. Long* has been engaged in creating books for preschoolers and beginning readers. He worked for over 20 years for Western Publishing Company as writer and editor in their juvenile division. Long was responsible for many of Western's Little Golden Books, enjoyed by countless numbers of small children. While at Western Publishing, he worked closely with Louis Untermeyer on *Poems for the Very Young* and authored a large number of read-to books. He also created for the juvenile education department *Getting Your Child Ready to Read* and *The First Big Step—Getting Ready for School.*

Long's many other works include the *Colour Library of Animal Books, Facts About the States,* and *The Story of Human Kind.*

ACKNOWLEDGMENTS:

Real-Life Heroes

TEXT

Raymond V. Hand, Jr.

ILLUSTRATIONS

John Gampert pp. 14–17, 33–36, 44–47, 55, 57, 70–72, 89–92
John Jones/Publishers' Graphics, Inc. pp. 22–23, 25, 41, 43, 59, 61–62, 81–84
Gary Lippincott/Publishers' Graphics, Inc. pp. 4–7, 18–21, 48, 50–51, 66–68, 77, 79–80, 85–88
John Rice/The Ivy League of Artists, Inc. pp. 8–10, 29, 31–32, 63, 65
David Rickman/Publishers' Graphics, Inc. pp. 11, 13, 37, 39, 52, 54
James Watling/Publishers' Graphics, Inc. pp. 26, 28, 73–75, 93, 95

America's Story

TEXT

Jack B. Long

ILLUSTRATIONS

Lloyd P. Birmingham p. 130
Bill Colrus/The Ivy League of Artists, Inc. pp. 102, 104, 141–143, 158–160, 189, 191, 217–219, 221
Ric Del Rossi/The Ivy League of Artists, Inc. pp. 119–120, 122, 149–151, 153, 167–169, 171
Bert Dodson/Publishers' Graphics, Inc. pp. 111–112, 162–165, 197–199, 201
John Gampert pp. 106–107, 109, 123–125, 145, 148, 180, 182–183, 207, 209–211
John Rice/The Ivy League of Artists, Inc. pp. 132–133, 135, 184, 186–187
David Rickman/Publishers' Graphics, Inc. pp. 98–101, 137, 139–140, 154–157, 176–177, 179, 202, 204–205
James Watling/Publishers' Graphics, Inc. pp. 115–117, 127, 129–131, 172, 174–175, 193, 195, 212, 214–215

Produced by The Hudson Group, Inc.
Art Direction by Pam Forde Graphics

Copyright 1994, 1993, 1992, 1991, 1990, 1989, 1987, 1984, 1982, 1979, 1973, 1968 by The Southwestern Company
Printed in the United States of America

Contents

Real-Life Heroes

America's Story

Real-Life Heroes

Joan of Arc
and the Power of
Fearlessness

A VERY LONG TIME AGO, in 1412, 80 years before Christopher Columbus discovered America, a girl was born in a village in northeastern France called Domremy. The proud parents, Jacques D'Arc and his wife Isabelle, named her Jeanne, or Joan as she is known in English. She was to become one of the most famous women who ever lived.

Joan was a bright and witty girl known for her gentleness and kindness. She was a great help to her family. She learned how to sew and to spin thread, but she never learned how to read or write.

Joan was a very religious girl. She was often found deep in prayer in the church at Domremy. Joan had much to pray for, because her country was being turned to ruins in a great war with England that came to be called the Hundred Years' War.

Henry VI, the king of England, claimed that he was the rightful ruler of France. He had the support of the French duke of Burgundy. But others claimed the crown for the French dauphin, Charles. The dauphin was the son of the French king, Charles VI, and heir to his throne.

Several times when Joan was growing up, she heard the sounds of battle raging near her little town. The English and their allies, the Burgundians, tried to defeat the supporters of the dauphin in northeastern France, but they never succeeded.

When Joan was about 13, a very strange thing happened to her. She began to hear the voices of Saint Michael, Saint Margaret, and Saint Catherine, the saints whose statues stood in the church at Domremy. Joan did not like to talk about her voices or what they told her, but she was convinced they were real.

When she was about 16, the voices told her to help Charles defeat the English and claim the crown of France.

Joan knew nothing about warfare, but she had faith in her voices and was a fearless young woman. She said goodby to her family and friends, and began her journey to the nearby town of Vaucouleurs to see the French commander there.

At first the commander laughed at Joan and sent her back home. But the voices urged her to try again and she returned to Vaucouleurs. Finally the commander sent her to see the dauphin.

Charles was impressed by this fearless young woman who announced that she was sent by God to defeat the English and make him king. But he wondered if she might be imagining her voices, or making up her story entirely.

Charles had Joan questioned by the wisest church officials he could find. They found no fault with her religious beliefs and could not shake her belief in her voices or in her mission.

At last Charles gave Joan a force of French soldiers. She led them to the city of Orléans, which was completely surrounded by the English.

The fall of Orléans would have been a great victory for the English, but Joan never doubted the outcome of the battle. The French soldiers took heart at the sight of this young woman in armor, standing fearlessly in the heat of battle and urging her troops to victory. In contest after contest, enemy strongholds fell to Joan, and soon the English were forced to retreat from Orléans.

Now Joan began to capture the English-held towns that stood in the path of her goal, the city of Reims, where all the French kings for a long time had been crowned.

The English were terrified by this girl in armor. She seemed to know more about making war than their finest generals and seemed to have no fear at all. One by one the towns surrendered to Joan.

Finally, the road to Reims was clear. Charles marched into the city at the head of a victorious army. The next day he was crowned Charles VII, king of France.

Joan urged Charles to continue the fight to free his country, but he was a cautious man and put off fighting. After months of waiting, Joan set out with a small force, but she found no more great victories. At the town of Compiègne she was captured by Burgundians and sold to the English. She was charged with being a witch.

Joan stood up fearlessly to the charges brought against her, especially the charge that her voices were false. Finally, she was sentenced to death.

Joan did not live to see her 20th birthday, but her fearlessness gave the French courage to continue their struggle. In time they forced the English to give up their claims and return to England. Today Joan of Arc is honored as one of the great heroines of France.

Haym Salomon
and the Power of
Generosity

ONE OF THE GREAT HEROES of the American Revolution never fired a shot and never led soldiers into battle. Yet without his help, America might not have gained its independence. Our nation's history would have been quite different.

Born in Poland, this generous man's name was Haym Salomon. His parents taught him to value education, to be proud of his Jewish heritage, and to love his country.

Haym Salomon traveled through Europe when he was a young man. During his travels he learned several languages and met many people. He returned home with valuable experience, new ideas, and a desire to help his country.

At that time, Poland was under the control of Russia, its powerful neighbor. Haym Salomon joined a group of Polish patriots who wanted to make Poland truly independent. But when the Russians crushed the independence movement, Salomon had to flee Poland for his life.

He came to New York City where he became a merchant. His business abilities, his understanding of people,

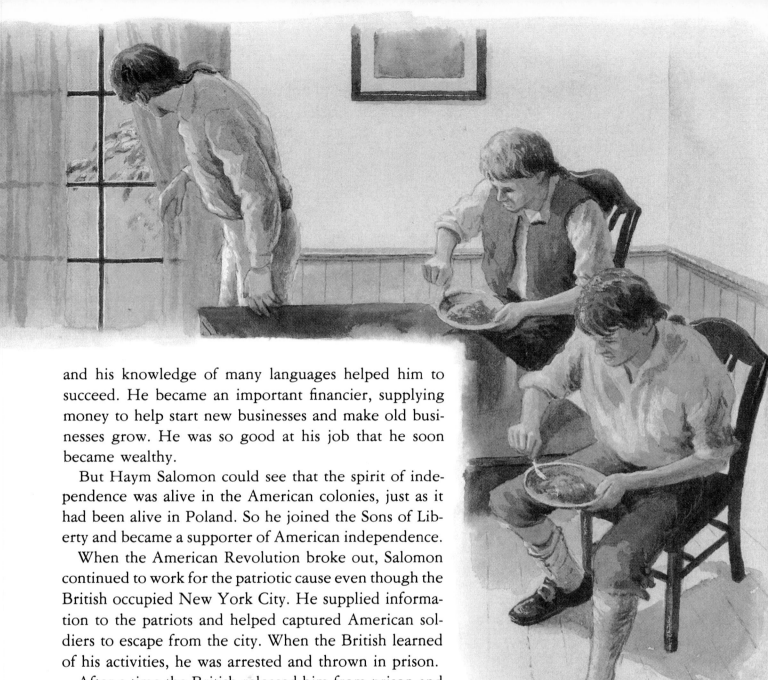

and his knowledge of many languages helped him to succeed. He became an important financier, supplying money to help start new businesses and make old businesses grow. He was so good at his job that he soon became wealthy.

But Haym Salomon could see that the spirit of independence was alive in the American colonies, just as it had been alive in Poland. So he joined the Sons of Liberty and became a supporter of American independence.

When the American Revolution broke out, Salomon continued to work for the patriotic cause even though the British occupied New York City. He supplied information to the patriots and helped captured American soldiers to escape from the city. When the British learned of his activities, he was arrested and thrown in prison.

After a time the British released him from prison and put him to work as a translator for a Hessian general. The Hessians were hired soldiers from Germany who were fighting for the British. Salomon used his new job to encourage many Hessian soldiers to resign from the army or to join the patriots.

Haym Salomon was again arrested. This time he was condemned to death. But he was able to bribe his jailer and escape to Philadelphia. He offered his services to the Continental Congress, but they were not accepted.

Salomon was not discouraged. He went into business again. In a short time he was one of the busiest financiers in Philadelphia. The French government selected him to handle all its financial affairs with the United States. For his generous services, Salomon charged nothing. That was his way of helping the patriotic cause.

Many times during the Revolution, the Continental Congress found itself in need of money. Haym Salomon was always ready to help. His generosity knew no limits. He lent the government large sums of money. He paid to equip many patriotic soldiers and made personal loans to officials so they could continue to work in the government. He lent money to Thomas Jefferson, James Madison, and others, at no profit to himself. He also helped feed the poor of Philadelphia during the darkest days of the war.

Haym Salomon's generosity helped the Americans pay for the war, keep the patriots' army in the field, secure the aid of the French, and gain American independence. Haym Salomon was truly one of the great heroes of the American Revolution.

Sacagawea
and the Power of
Trust

IN THE SPRING OF 1804 Meriwether Lewis and William Clark led an expedition up the Missouri River and across the Rocky Mountains. Their goal was to explore the newly purchased Louisiana Territory, a huge tract of land stretching from the Mississippi River to the Pacific Ocean. The year before, President Thomas Jefferson had bought the land from France. The Louisiana Territory, which more than doubled the size of the United States, was largely unknown. Jefferson organized the Lewis and Clark Expedition, as it came to be known, to seek a trail to the Pacific, discover and record new plants and animals, and learn about the Indian tribes who lived there.

In late 1804 the expedition stopped to spend the winter at a Mandan Indian village in what is now North Dakota. There they arranged for the men, animals, and equipment they would need when they were ready to move west, as soon as the weather turned warm. But they also needed someone who knew the language of the Shoshone Indians, whose land they would cross on their way to the Pacific. That is how they came to employ an Indian woman named Sacagawea.

The daughter of a Shoshone Indian chief, Sacagawea had been captured in a raid by Hidatsa Indians. She had grown up among the Hidatsas and became the wife of Toussaint Charbonneau, a French-Canadian trapper.

The two leaders discovered that the only person who could speak the language of the Shoshones was Sacagawea. So they hired Charbonneau as an interpreter after he agreed to take Sacagawea along with him on their expedition into the new American frontier.

Sacagawea was only about 16 years old. Though she had just given birth to her first baby, a boy named Jean Baptiste, she was happy to join the expedition.

Lewis and Clark put all their trust in Sacagawea because they needed help from the Shoshone Indians. Without horses from the Shoshones, they would have no way to carry their equipment and supplies across the Rocky Mountains.

Very soon the two leaders learned they had trusted the right person. When a boat tipped over and filled with water, Sacagawea calmly and quickly saved almost all of the things that had fallen out of the boat, including the records of the expedition.

As they moved west, Sacagawea began to recognize places she had seen as a child. Then one day a large group of Shoshone Indians came to where the expedition was camped. Sacagawea suddenly saw a girl she had played with as a child. The two smiled and laughed and hugged each other. Sacagawea was home at last.

Sacagawea soon found her brother, who was now a chief. Her eyes filled with tears of happiness.

With Sacagawea's help as translator, the expedition was able to get the horses it needed. Some of the Shoshone Indians were hired as guides.

Sacagawea carried her baby all the way west, and all the way back. She helped make the mission a success in many ways. She found wild foods for the explorers to eat. Many times they were treated as friends by the Indians simply because Sacagawea and her baby were traveling with them.

In every way, Sacagawea showed that Meriwether Lewis and William Clark had placed their trust in the right person.

Robert E. Lee
and the Power of
Character

WHEN ROBERT E. LEE WAS BORN in Virginia in 1807, the United States was still a young country. Because the U.S. Constitution had been in effect for only 18 years, America's leaders were still uncertain about how much authority the federal government had over the states. The Supreme Court had not yet settled the conflict between states' rights and the rights of the federal government. It was a question that would be settled partly by the Civil War (also known as the War Between the States).

Robert E. Lee's father, Henry Lee, had been a brave and victorious cavalry commander in the Revolutionary War; he was known to most people as Light-Horse Harry Lee. He had also served as governor of Virginia. It was Henry Lee who had said of George Washington, "First in war, first in peace, and first in the hearts of his countrymen." But by the time his son Robert was born, Light-Horse Harry Lee's days of glory had come and gone. He had fallen into debt because of some bad business deals, and the family had to leave their plantation home, Stratford, when Robert was about four years old.

Robert E. Lee grew up in a small brick house in the city of Alexandria, Virginia. Though a quiet, gentle boy, he was very strong and quite fearless. Even as a young schoolboy, he began to show all the good qualities that form a strong person's character.

Lee's hero was George Washington, whose honesty, sense of justice, and devotion to duty had made him a hero to the whole nation. Lee learned to love his country and to love the state of Virginia, which was his home state and the home state of George Washington and Thomas Jefferson.

When Lee was eleven years old, his father died. Since his two older brothers had already set out to make their way in the world, he was the only son left to help his family.

Love of family was one of the qualities Robert E. Lee learned very early in his life. He quietly accepted his new responsibilities. He tended the family garden, took care of the house and stable, and cared for his mother, who was in ill health.

Several years later Robert E. Lee entered the United States Military Academy at West Point. He was an excellent student, graduating from the academy second in his class. He was appointed a lieutenant in the U.S. Army.

Lee served as an Army engineer, working at building and repairing forts, improving the harbor at St. Louis,

and removing obstacles to shipping up and down the Mississippi River. He also served during the Mexican War, was the superintendent of West Point, and commanded a cavalry regiment in Texas.

Meanwhile, the storm clouds of civil war were building in the United States over slavery and states' rights. The two issues caused great mistrust between the industrial North and the agricultural South. Shortly after Abraham Lincoln was elected President in 1860, the Southern states declared they were leaving, or seceding from, the United States to form the Confederate States of America. The Civil War had begun.

When Robert E. Lee was offered command of the Union Army, he faced the most difficult decision he would ever make. He loved his country deeply but he believed his first loyalty was to his beloved Virginia. Like many other Virginians, he thought slavery was wrong and was not in favor of secession. So Lee decided that if Virginia stayed in the Union, he would support the Union cause.

But Virginia seceded from the Union. With great sadness, Lee resigned from the U.S. Army. Two months later he became a general in the Confederate Army.

For four years Lee followed the course his character and sense of duty had set out for him. He was a brilliant officer, and time and again he led his troops to victory over stronger Union forces. He became the chief military adviser to Confederate President Jefferson Davis,

and eventually was made commander in chief of the Confederate Army.

But time was on the side of the Union, which had more of everything—more people, more factories, and more money to spend on war. In April of 1865, Lee's army, hungry and worn out, was trapped by the Union Army. Lee surrendered to General Ulysses S. Grant, and the Civil War was over.

Robert E. Lee had showed that it is character that makes a person great. He had followed his sense of duty, had fought fearlessly, and had always tried to do what was right. He earned the respect of friend and foe alike.

Harriet Tubman
and the Power of
Helping

HARRIET TUBMAN WAS BORN in a small cabin on a plantation in Maryland about 1821. Her parents, who were slaves, could not read or write, so they did not record her exact birth date. They named their little girl Araminta and, while she was growing up, everyone called her Minta, or Minty.

Little Minty was put to work when she was about five years old. At first her master hired her out to other white families. Though she was just a child, she had to work very hard.

At one house where Minty was sent to work she was told to dust and sweep a room. She did not know how to do it because she had never done it before but she tried her best. When the lady of the house checked Minty's work, she became so angry she beat the little girl.

Minty also had to care for the children of the people she was sent to live with. Her job was to watch the children all the time. If they made too much noise, she would be beaten.

Minty hated the work she was forced to do but, even more, she hated the way she was treated. The people she worked for would always become angry with her and send her back to the plantation.

Finally, Minty asked her master not to send her away anymore. She asked to work in the fields. It was very hard work, but at least she would be out in the fresh air with the world of nature all around her.

So she went into the fields, working from sunrise to sunset with the other field hands. She became very strong from the hard work. She learned many things. But she never learned to accept slavery.

Freedom! Minty never learned to read or write, but she knew deep in her heart what the word freedom means. She learned about freedom from her father, who showed her the North Star, and told her that if people walked far enough and kept the North Star always in front of them, they could get to a land of freedom. He also taught her how to walk through woods and across fields without being seen or heard and how to find food growing wild, ready for picking.

One day Minty decided she wanted to be called Harriet, which was her mother's name. When she became a young woman, Harriet married John Tubman. John Tubman was black, but he was a free man. Harriet longed to be free too and she told John she wanted to follow the North Star to freedom. But he did not want to leave Maryland.

She set off by herself on the dangerous journey north to freedom. She knew that if she were caught, she would probably be sold down the river, that is, sent down the Mississippi River to a new master, far from her family.

On her way north Harriet Tubman learned about the Underground Railroad. It was not a real railroad. It was an organization of good people who, because they knew slavery was wrong, were helping slaves escape to freedom. These people helping slaves escape were called conductors and station masters, just as if they were working for a railroad, and each stop along the way was called a station.

When Harriet Tubman reached freedom in the North, she did not forget that her family was still in slavery back in Maryland. She also remembered and knew she could count on more help from those kind men and women who had helped her escape. She decided to go back south secretly and lead her family and friends to freedom—along the Underground Railroad.

Harriet Tubman made many trips south and conducted hundreds of slaves north along the Underground Railroad. Every trip was more dangerous than the last because her successes were turning her into a legend. No longer was she called Harriet Tubman. Now she was called Moses because, like Moses in the Bible, she was leading her people to freedom.

A large reward was offered for her capture, but she was not afraid. Harriet thought that helping others along the road to freedom was well worth the risk. She was never caught.

When the Civil War began, Harriet Tubman worked as a nurse and a scout with the Union Army on the coast of South Carolina. She helped free many more slaves.

Harriet Tubman always remembered the people who had helped her to become free. In turn, the people she helped always remembered her, especially for the bravery she showed in helping others.

Maria Mitchell
and the Power of
Persistence

A HUNDRED AND FIFTY YEARS AGO Nantucket, an island off the coast of Massachusetts, was the home port of most of America's whaling ships. The captains of Nantucket sailed their ships to the farthest oceans, hunting whales. They brought back whale oil and other important products that were very important to people in those days.

While at sea the captains had only the position of the stars in the night sky to tell them where they were and how far they had sailed. Since getting back home safely depended on the sea captains' knowledge of the stars and planets, it was natural that the people of Nantucket would be interested in astronomy, the study of the stars and planets and their movements in the heavens.

Maria Mitchell was the daughter of the principal of the public school in Nantucket. Her father was deeply interested in astronomy. He had taught himself so much about the stars that the ship captains would ask him to test the instruments they used to measure the positions of the stars. It was very important that the instruments worked correctly.

While still a girl, Maria began helping her father check these instruments. Mr. Mitchell would measure the position of a star with an instrument, then check its readings against a printed list of readings. Maria thought such work was a wonderful way to learn numbers and arithmetic. It was a fun way to learn.

Maria and her father would look at the stars through his telescope, and the little girl soon knew their names and their movement across the sky.

Maria Mitchell was interested in everything, but especially mathematics, science, and astronomy. She did not consider herself a bright student, but she was persistent. She studied carefully and steadily, not giving up until she learned what she wanted to know.

When she got older Maria became the librarian of Nantucket's public library. Being a librarian was a wonderful job. Maria enjoyed helping people, especially young people. When she was alone at the library, she could spend much time studying more about mathematics and astronomy.

Every free evening Maria joined her father at the telescope he had set up on the roof of their house. Together they made observations and collected readings.

One day Maria learned that the king of Denmark had offered a gold medal to the first person to find any comet that had not yet been discovered. Maria decided to find a new comet and win the gold medal. Patiently, she began the long search.

Every night she would go out to the telescope she and her father used, and search the night sky for her unknown comet. Night after night she observed the beauty of the stars and planets, but she could find no new comet. But she never gave up. She believed that with persistence she would find her comet.

The days passed. The months passed. The seasons passed. Maria did not give up her search.

Then on October 1, 1847, Maria Mitchell found her comet, just a little above the North Star. Filled with excitement, she showed her father what she had seen. He looked through the telescope at it. Then he turned to her. Yes, he said, yes, indeed. It was a comet!

Soon the news spread of Maria Mitchell's discovery. Astronomers in America and Europe agreed that it was a new comet, and they named it after Maria Mitchell.

One day a package arrived in Nantucket for Maria. It was her gold medal sent across the ocean to her from the king of Denmark.

Maria Mitchell's persistence in her search for a comet started her on an exciting life. She was the first woman member of the American Academy of Arts and Sciences. Later she had a brilliant career as the first professor of astronomy at Vassar College.

Louisa May Alcott
and the Power of
Family

WHEN LOUISA MAY ALCOTT was a young girl growing up in Concord, Massachusetts, in the 1840's, she liked to daydream. Her imagination gave her an endless supply of exciting adventures and most of them had happy endings.

Louisa's father, Bronson Alcott, was a teacher and philosopher. He was known for his advanced ideas about many things, especially about education. He would travel about the country to deliver his lectures, but they earned him only a little money. He had no sense at all when it came to business.

The Alcott family seemed always to be in debt, which made life hard for Louisa, her three sisters, and their mother. Yet Louisa, of course, loved her father dearly and thought that in his own independent way he was a great man.

Louisa's talent for dreaming about adventure, romance, and happiness was matched by her skill at writing. She wrote poems and letters and kept a diary. When she was 16 she wrote her first short story.

About this time Louisa decided that she had to find work to help her family. First she tried teaching. She worked also as a housekeeper and then as a seamstress. She liked sewing because it gave her time and periods of quiet to think out her stories.

Louisa's first story, the one she had written when she was 16, was published in 1852, when she was 20. She did not think it was great, but it was a start. She was hoping to earn enough money from writing to help her family. In the next few years she wrote many stories for the weekly newspapers, but she was paid very little for her stories. Her goal seemed as far away as ever.

When the Civil War began, Louisa decided to become a nurse. She traveled to Washington, D.C., where she went to work in a Union hospital. The sight of suffering and sickness, the long hours, and the hard work weakened her so much that she soon fell ill. She returned to her Concord home to recover, but she never regained her health completely.

Louisa's terrible experiences, however, led to the beginning of her success as a writer. In 1863 her letters home were printed in a book called *Hospital Sketches,* which sold well. The next year her first novel, a book entitled *Moods*, was published.

Louisa still had to help her family. Though she continued to write, she took a job as editor of a magazine for children in order to earn more money.

Then a publisher asked her to write a novel for girls. Louisa did not like the idea at first, but in 1868 she decided to write a story she had been planning for many years, a story based on her own family.

She began writing for long hours every day. In six weeks she finished the first part of *Little Women,* a novel about a family named March. It is a love story, a Civil War story, and a family story. When it was published, readers from all over the country rushed to buy it. It took Louisa six weeks to finish the second part. Again, people flocked to the bookstores to buy their copies.

Everyone was talking about the March family. Adults liked the novel as much as children did. People stopped on street corners to talk about the adventures of the March daughters, Meg, Jo, Beth, and Amy, who were modeled after the Alcott daughters, Anna, Louisa, Elizabeth, and May. Even its title, *Little Women,* came from the Alcott family, for that was what Bronson Alcott lovingly called his daughters.

Louisa May Alcott was suddenly a famous author. For the first time in her life she had more money than she needed. She paid off all her family's debts and put some money away for the future. Then she and May, her youngest sister, went on a trip to Europe.

Louisa May Alcott continued the adventures of the March family in two more books, *Little Men* and *Jo's Boys.* The three novels about the March family were her most successful books, probably because she modeled her make-believe people after those she knew and loved best, her own family and friends. Her tales about the joys and sorrows of family life are just as alive today as they were a hundred years ago.

Booker T. Washington
and the Power of
Education

IN THE FALL OF 1872 Booker T. Washington arrived unannounced at the door of the Hampton Institute, in Hampton, Virginia. The 16-year-old boy had walked for many days to reach this school. He was hungry and tired. But his heart was filled with happiness and hope for the future. More than anything, he wanted to go to this school in order to get a good education.

Booker was born in 1856 on a plantation in Virginia. His mother, a slave, was the plantation cook and her kitchen was the family's cabin. Booker's bed, which he shared with his brother and sister, was a pile of rags on the bare earth floor.

As soon as he was strong enough, Booker worked on the plantation. It was a very hard life.

When Booker was five years old the Civil War broke out. The conflict between the Union and the Confederacy made life on the plantation even worse. Then, at the war's end, Booker, his family, and all the slaves on the plantation were told they were free to go anywhere they chose and to work at whatever they wanted.

Booker and his family moved to Malden, West Virginia, to live with Booker's stepfather. There, Booker went to work at a furnace where salt was made. The work was hard. Many times the boy began work before sunrise and finished after sunset.

About this time Booker got his first book, a blue-covered spelling book. He taught himself the letters of the alphabet and went to school when he could. But he still had to work to help his family, so sometimes he had school lessons at night and sometimes during the day.

On his first day at school his teacher asked him what his name was. He had always been called by one name, Booker, but the other children had two names, so he chose a second name, Washington. Later he learned his mother had named him Booker Taliaferro, so he put all the names together and called himself Booker Taliaferro Washington.

After staying for a while at the salt furnace, Booker went to work in a coal mine. One day he heard two miners talking about a new school in Virginia for black students. Then and there the boy made a big decision. He promised himself he would go to that school.

He found a job in the house of a white family. The lady of the house was strict, insisting that everything be kept clean and tidy at all times. Booker worked very hard. Pretty soon he and the lady became good friends. But always he kept in mind the school in Virginia. Its name was Hampton Institute.

So Booker T. Washington made his way to Hampton Institute. It was a long journey. He worked along the way to pay for his food. He slept outdoors in the cold to save money. When he arrived at the school, he had exactly 50 cents in his pocket.

At first the head teacher did not want to admit him as a student. But she gave him a broom and told him to sweep out a classroom. He swept the room three times and dusted it four times. The teacher was so impressed, she accepted him as a student. She also gave him a job as a janitor to help him pay his expenses.

At Hampton Institute Booker Washington worked and studied as hard as he could. He put all his effort into getting a good education. When his schooling was completed he became a teacher and, after a while, he returned to teach at Hampton Institute.

In 1881 Booker T. Washington was asked to organize a new school for blacks in Tuskegee, Alabama. When he got to Tuskegee, he found the school was just a single wooden building next to the local church.

He set to work. Borrowing some money, he bought an abandoned farm. Then he built a kiln for making bricks and put the students to work building their own classrooms and dormitories. At this new school he put his ideas about education into practice. Though he wanted

his students to learn from books, he also wanted them, by working with their hands, to learn practical skills that could earn them a decent living and respect.

Booker T. Washington worked tirelessly for many years to expand and improve Tuskegee Institute. He traveled across the country, speaking about the value of education. He wrote many articles and a number of books, including his own life story, *Up from Slavery.*

Under his guidance Tuskegee Institute became a great center of learning known throughout the world. Many of its graduates have built careers in business, science, the arts, law, and medicine. Others have found success in farming, manufacturing, and construction.

Their achievements were made possible by Booker T. Washington, whose love for education inspired his whole life.

Thomas Edison
and the Power of
Work

WHEN THOMAS ALVA EDISON was growing up in
Port Huron, Michigan, in the 1850's, he showed great
curiosity about everything around him. Even when he
was very young, he liked to learn by experimenting. As
he grew older, the pleasure he got from experimenting
became deeper as his knowledge increased.

But Edison was not a good student. In fact, he attended
school for only short periods of time. Most of his schooling came from his mother. Having been a teacher, she
decided he would learn a good deal more at home under
her guidance than at school.

And how he did learn! History, mathematics, geogra-
phy and, best of all, science. He read everything that
came into his hands. Books on chemistry were his favor-
ites, but he did more than just read them. He tried many
of the experiments they described to prove to himself
that the facts he had learned in books were really true.

Chemicals for experiments cost money, and there were
so many experiments to be tried. When he was about
twelve years old, Thomas Edison went into business selling candy and newspapers on the train that ran from Port
Huron to Detroit, about 60 miles away. He also found
time to edit and publish his own weekly newspaper,

phonograph

movie projector

which he printed on a small press that he kept in a corner of the baggage car. He also set up a homemade laboratory in the baggage car. When he was not selling to the passengers or working on his newspaper, he worked on his scientific experiments.

One day Edison was given the chance to learn how to be a telegraph operator. The telegraph, which had been invented only a few years earlier, used electricity to send signals along wires from one place to another. He had to practice every day for months to learn these signals of the Morse code, made up of dots and dashes that sounded like fast and slow clicking sounds. With the Morse code all kinds of messages and news were sent from one end of the country to the other by means of electricity. Edison became as fascinated by electricity as he had been by chemistry.

In a few years Edison was working as a first-class telegrapher. When he was not operating the telegraph, he was hard at work inventing new devices that greatly improved the telegraph system.

Then Thomas Edison turned to inventing full time. He had so many ideas for inventions that he knew he would have to work very hard to complete them all.

In 1876 Edison built a laboratory at Menlo Park, New Jersey. There he gathered together the best craftsmen and scientists he could find to put them to work in what he called his "idea factory."

A year later Edison introduced his first great invention, the phonograph. For the first time people could record, and later replay, speeches, music, or any other sounds they wished to preserve forever. This was a wonderful invention and earned Edison much praise, but the inventor had little time for honors. He quickly turned to another project.

In 1879, after many months of hard work, Edison demonstrated his greatest invention, the incandescent lamp, or electric light bulb. Its bright, pleasant light changed the way people lived forever.

Soon Edison was hard at work inventing all the things that were needed to make electric lighting available to anyone who wanted it. Generators, power lines, fuses, switches, electric meters—all had to be invented before the first electric power station opened for business in New York City.

At first only a small part of New York was lighted using the Edison electric system, but within a few years electric lighting was being installed in towns and cities across the nation and around the world.

Such success would have been enough for most people, but Edison just kept on working. In 1887 he built a new, larger laboratory in West Orange, New Jersey, and continued his work. He improved the phonograph and experimented with motion pictures. He even built the world's first movie studio.

Thomas Edison once described genius as "one percent inspiration and ninety-nine percent perspiration." He also said, "I never did anything worth doing by accident, nor did any of my inventions come by accident; they came by work."

Edison was awarded 1093 patents for his inventions. Because of his natural curiosity and belief in hard work, our world today is a much better place in which to live.

Walter Reed
and the Power of
Dedication

WALTER REED WAS STILL A BOY when he decided what he wanted to do with his life. More than anything else, he wanted to become a doctor and help ease the pain and suffering of other people.

Born in Virginia, Walter Reed was the son of a Methodist minister. He grew up during the Civil War. When he was 15 years old, Walter entered the University of Virginia, where his dedication to study was so complete that when he was only 17 he was admitted to the university's medical school. In one year he completed his medical studies, passed his examination, and was awarded his medical degree. At 18 he was the youngest graduate in the school's history.

Dr. Reed practiced in New York City and in the borough of Brooklyn for several years. But he was not happy. He had seen too much suffering and often felt unable to help those who were sick. He was also discouraged because some of his fellow doctors were poorly trained and cared little for their patients.

Then Walter Reed made a decision that changed his life. He joined the Army Medical Corps and became an Army surgeon. His dedication to his patients and to the field of medicine earned him a promotion to captain, and then to major. He was transferred to Baltimore, Maryland, to continue his studies, and then to Washington, D.C., to teach at the Army Medical School.

During the Spanish-American War, American soldiers were sent to fight in Cuba. There they found that their deadliest enemy was not the Spanish army, but a disease called yellow fever.

The soldiers called it yellow jack. Nobody knew where it came from or how it spread from one person to another. For centuries, outbreaks of yellow fever had killed tens of thousands of people. Now it swept across Cuba, again killing thousands.

Major Reed had already shown that typhoid fever was spread mainly by the common fly. Measures to get rid of flies greatly reduced the number of new typhoid cases. Now he was asked to find out what caused yellow fever and how it was spread.

He went to work with determination. He traveled to Cuba where he learned everything he could about the epidemic. He became convinced that yellow fever was spread by a certain kind of mosquito, *Aedes aegypti,* as scientists call it. He believed the mosquito would bite a person suffering from yellow fever and then would infect healthy persons when it bit them. It was a good theory, but Walter Reed needed to prove he was right.

To test his theory, Major Reed wanted to let an infected mosquito bite him. But members of his medical team refused to let him do it. His life could not be risked, they said. After all, it was his experiment. How could they continue if he died?

Dr. James Carroll, a member of Reed's team, volunteered to be bitten by an infected mosquito. A soldier, Private William E. Dean, also volunteered. They fell ill, but both recovered.

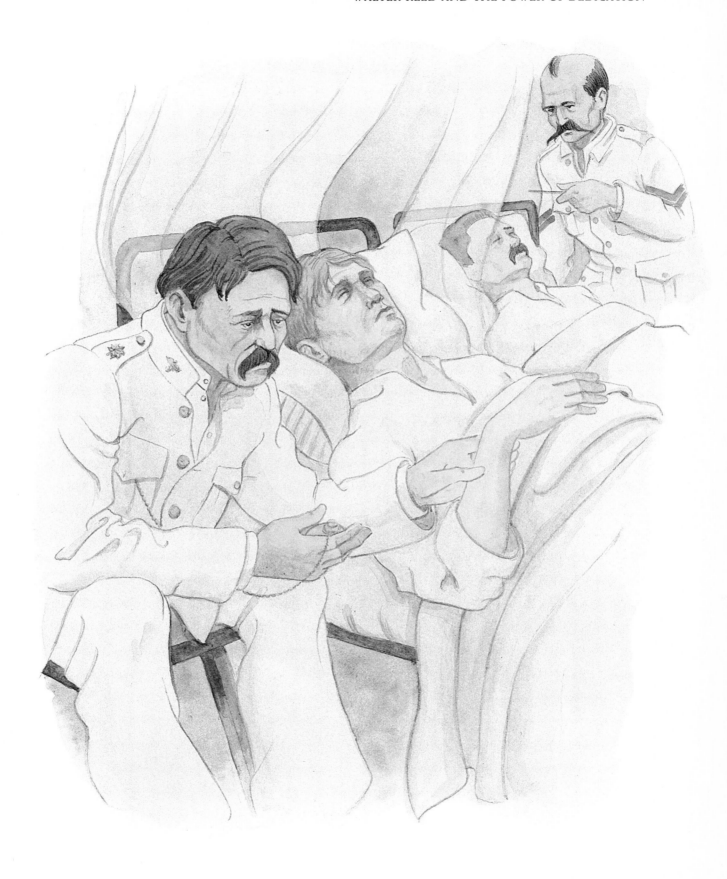

Dr. Jesse Lazear, another member of the team, was accidentally bitten by a mosquito and died nine days later. Major Reed was deeply saddened by his death and he became even more determined to defeat yellow fever.

Though Walter Reed knew he was on the right path to controlling yellow fever, he needed to prove beyond doubt that the mosquito, and nothing else, spread the disease. The only way to prove this was to put a group of volunteers where they could not come in contact with the disease in any way, and then let them be bitten by infected mosquitoes. If they fell ill, he would know the mosquitoes were responsible.

A special camp was built to conduct the tests. A number of volunteers were bitten by the mosquitoes, and soon they fell ill. Dr. Reed worked day and night to make sure the experiment was done correctly. He worried over each patient who became ill, and made sure each was well cared for. They all recovered.

Another group of volunteers, separated from the others, were not bitten by the mosquitoes. Instead, they slept in bedsheets used by yellow fever victims, wore their clothes, and used their towels. But none of them became ill.

Reed now had the evidence he needed. The mosquitoes did carry the disease. The Army began to destroy the mosquitoes and their breeding grounds. Soon there were very few new yellow fever cases.

Through their dedication, Dr. Walter Reed and his team had defeated one of humanity's deadliest enemies, and had made important new discoveries in the war against disease.

Jane Addams
and the Power of
Sharing

JANE ADDAMS WAS BORN only a few months before the Civil War began and just two months before Abraham Lincoln was elected President of the United States. Her father, a prosperous businessman and a state senator from Illinois, knew Lincoln well and shared his belief that all people should be free to enjoy the fruits of their own labor. When the Civil War began, John Addams organized a company of soldiers called the "Addams Guards" and went off to fight for the Union.

Like many other children, Jane Addams believed her father was the greatest man in the world. Even as a young girl, she would talk with him about the problems and puzzles she found in life.

When she was seven years old, she and her father traveled from their home in Cedarville to visit a mill located in a very poor section of a neighboring town. Jane noticed that the children lived in small, run-down houses packed so closely together there was hardly any place to play.

Jane asked her father why people lived that way, but his explanation did not satisfy her. She told him that when she grew up she would live in a big, beautiful house but that it would not be located among other big, beautiful houses in the country. It would be right near poor little houses like the ones she saw around her. Then she could share the beauty and comfort of her house with those who were not so rich as she was.

Though Jane Addams lived in a beautiful house and her father was a respected man in Illinois, her life was far from perfect. She had a problem with her spine that caused her head to tilt to one side, so she thought herself ugly. Sometimes she even tried to conceal the fact that she was John Addams's daughter so as not to cause him any embarrassment at having such an "Ugly Duckling" child. Her father never knew this, of course, or he would have told his daughter that she was not ugly at all and that he loved her just as she was.

As Jane grew up she never forgot that many people live in hunger, poverty, and sadness. She decided that her life's work would be to help make their lives better.

She went to Philadelphia to study medicine, but her spine problem forced her to leave school and have an operation. It took her a long time to recover. Several years passed while Jane Addams struggled to decide what to do with her life.

One day, while traveling in Europe with her friend Ellen Gates Starr, Jane Addams decided that she did not have to be a doctor to help people. She told Ellen of her idea to live among poor people and share with them the good things life had brought to her. She could help them learn about art and music, help them learn new skills, and help them with other problems they might have. Ellen liked the idea very much, and the two women started right away to plan what they would do.

In 1889 Jane and Ellen moved into Hull House, a big old mansion in a very poor section of Chicago. There they started many projects to help the working people of their neighborhood. Soon enough, children and their parents were coming to Hull House for classes, reading

groups, games, lectures, and all sorts of enjoyable and useful activities. Whenever any of the people had problems, they would go to Jane Addams. She shared her knowledge, experience, and money unselfishly in order to help them.

Jane Addams began a long campaign to provide better housing and better living conditions for poor people. She worked to get child labor laws passed to protect young people who had to take jobs to help their families. She worked to get women the right to vote. She worked to bring peace to the world. And she wrote many books telling what she and her friends had learned about helping others.

In 1931 Jane Addams was given one of the most important awards in the world, the Nobel Peace Prize. She had brought hope, beauty, and happiness into the lives of everyone around her simply by sharing her life with them.

Theodore Roosevelt
and the Power of
Leadership

WHEN THEODORE ROOSEVELT was growing up he thought he might like to become a scientist. The Civil War had just ended so it was natural that he would be interested in military history. At this early age he showed little interest in politics. He probably never dreamed that one day he would become President of the United States.

Theodore was a bright boy. He was constantly amazing his parents and other adults with his knowledge of animals and plants. But he was sickly. He had asthma, which often gave him trouble in breathing. He also had poor eyesight so he did not go to public school with other children. Instead, his parents hired private teachers, or tutors, to guide his education.

But young Theodore had great determination. He began to exercise every day, building up his strength. His progress was very slow, but as year followed year he began to turn his weakness into strength.

By the time he graduated from Harvard University, Roosevelt was full of life and energy. It was then that he was drawn to politics. He was elected to the New York State legislature, where he led a fight against corruption in politics and business in the state.

Then tragedy struck. Theodore Roosevelt's mother and wife both died. Roosevelt turned away from politics. He went to the Dakota Territory, where he raised cattle and wrote books. After two years there he returned to New York City and entered public life once again, quickly regaining his position as a leader in the fight against political corruption.

During the Spanish-American War, Roosevelt helped organize a volunteer cavalry force that became famous as the Rough Riders. In Cuba, Colonel Roosevelt showed he was a courageous leader in what came to be known as the Battle of San Juan Hill. Roosevelt led his troops in a charge up nearby Kettle Hill, and then helped American troops capture San Juan Hill from the Spanish forces.

When Roosevelt returned to New York, he was a national hero. In 1899 he became governor of New York.

In 1900 the Republican Party chose William McKinley as its Presidential candidate and Theodore Roosevelt as its Vice Presidential candidate.

When McKinley and Roosevelt were elected in November, the politicians who had opposed Roosevelt's reform-minded leadership were pleased that, at last, he had been put in a position that had very little real power. Even Roosevelt wondered if his career in politics had come to a quiet end.

Then, in the summer of 1901, President McKinley was shot. On September 14 McKinley died and Theodore Roosevelt was sworn in as the 26th President of the United States.

Roosevelt turned his enormous capacity for leadership to bringing a new standard of honesty in government, establishing a movement that became known as the Square Deal. He also worked to rebuild the Navy and establish the United States as a leading power in the world.

For many years the United States had wanted to build a canal that would link the Atlantic and Pacific oceans. The French had tried to build such a canal across Panama, which was then part of Colombia, but they had failed. Roosevelt pushed for a canal treaty with Colombia. The treaty was approved by the United States but Colombia voted it down.

When a group of people in Panama declared its independence from Colombia, Roosevelt immediately sent an American gunboat to protect the new government,

which quickly signed a new canal treaty with the United States. Many people were outraged by what they called Roosevelt's "gunboat diplomacy," but he was determined to have the canal built.

Theodore Roosevelt directed every stage in the planning and building of the Panama Canal. Under his leadership, the best American engineers, businessmen, mechanics, doctors, and manufacturers worked together to complete one of the greatest engineering projects in history.

Later he sent the American fleet on a two-year cruise around the world. This display of American strength and leadership put the United States for the first time on an equal footing with world powers. The fleet returned to the United States in 1909, shortly before Roosevelt stepped down from the presidency and returned to private life.

Theodore Roosevelt's strong leadership made the Panama Canal a reality, helped bring about important reforms in politics and business, and gave the United States a commanding position in world affairs. Few would question that he was one of America's greatest presidents.

Albert Einstein
and the Power of
Creativity

FROM EARLIEST TIMES people have tried to discover the natural laws of the universe and our own world. Isaac Newton, the famous English mathematician, made one of the greatest contributions to our understanding when he explained how the planets stay in orbit around the sun and how comets and stars move in space. He also explained how such natural forces as gravity and friction control the motion of objects on Earth. His explanations came to be called Newton's laws of motion. Because of these laws, modern science could develop.

But as scientists learned more and more, they found that Newton's laws were not quite perfect. They did not explain some things exactly enough. It became clear to many scientists that someone would have to find a new, creative way to describe the way the universe works.

Albert Einstein was born more than a hundred years ago in the city of Ulm, in southern Germany. He grew up at an exciting time, when new scientific discoveries were being made almost daily.

Albert was an observant boy. He liked to watch carefully what was happening around him, the motion of waves on a lake, the drift of clouds in the sky, the bending of tree branches in the breeze, the beauty of a rainbow. Whatever he watched told him something about how things move and change. Every experience had something new to teach him.

One day when he was five years old, Albert Einstein saw something that was different from anything he had seen before. His father showed him a compass. The compass had a needle that pointed out which direction is north. No matter how much his father shook the compass to get the needle spinning, as soon as he stopped, the needle would come to a halt and point to north every time.

Albert was amazed. It was almost like magic. There were no springs or gears in the compass that made the needle move. There was just the pointer needle, balanced delicately so that it could turn in a full circle.

The boy could not understand what made the needle act that way. It was as if some power made the needle point to the north. He could not feel this power, he could not hear it, he could not see it. His father called it magnetism but could not explain it. He wondered what magnetism is.

Albert's discovery that there are invisible forces at work in the world made a deep impression on him. It made him create in his mind many kinds of explanations to show why things behave the way they do.

As he grew older, his interest in mathematics and science grew as well. By the time he was 17, he knew more about these subjects than most adults. He saw clearly that the latest experiments with light and with electricity gave results that did not quite agree with Newton's laws. He knew that it would take lots of creativity and imagination to produce a better understanding of the universe.

Einstein finished his schooling and took a job at the Patent Office in Berne, Switzerland. Now he was able to write down the ideas he had stored away in his mind.

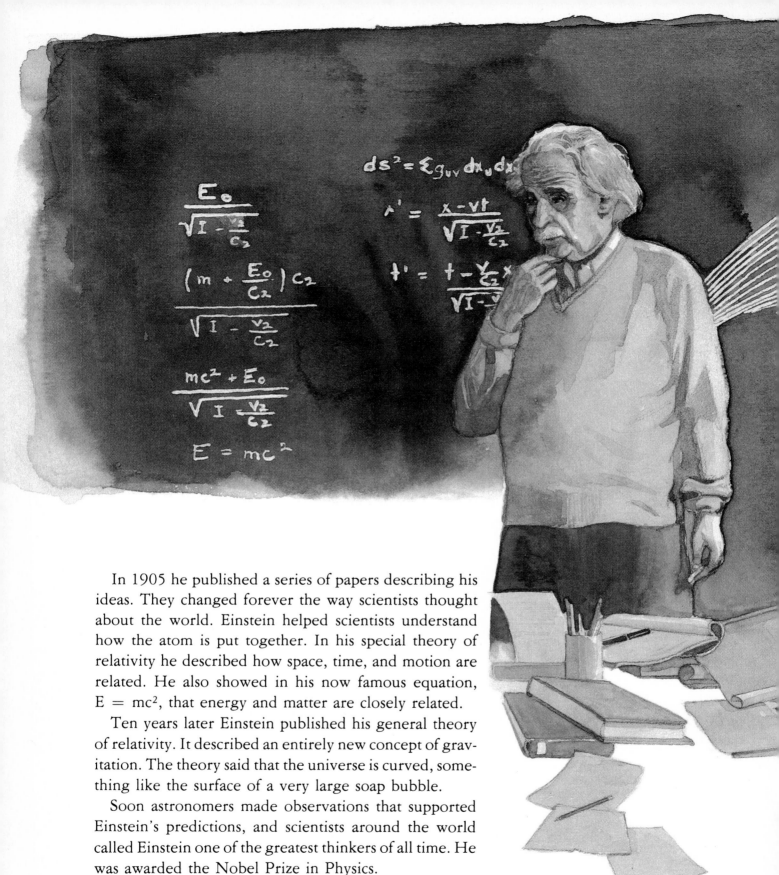

In 1905 he published a series of papers describing his ideas. They changed forever the way scientists thought about the world. Einstein helped scientists understand how the atom is put together. In his special theory of relativity he described how space, time, and motion are related. He also showed in his now famous equation, $E = mc^2$, that energy and matter are closely related.

Ten years later Einstein published his general theory of relativity. It described an entirely new concept of gravitation. The theory said that the universe is curved, something like the surface of a very large soap bubble.

Soon astronomers made observations that supported Einstein's predictions, and scientists around the world called Einstein one of the greatest thinkers of all time. He was awarded the Nobel Prize in Physics.

50

Albert Einstein's creativity gave scientists a new way to understand the mysteries of very small things, like atoms, and of very large things, like space. His genius made our world of nuclear power and space travel possible.

Marie Curie
and the Power of
Curiosity

MARYA SKLODOWSKA WAS BORN in Warsaw, the capital city of Poland, about 120 years ago. In future years the whole world would come to know her as the greatest scientist Marie Curie.

At school Marya was always the smartest student in her class. She liked especially to read. She read adventure stories, poems, history books, and science books. She was curious about everything. It seemed she never forgot anything. Her mind was like a sponge for facts.

Her father was a teacher of mathematics and physics and had many books about science. He let Marya read as many of the books as she wanted. She also liked to look at the delicate pieces of scientific equipment he kept in a large glass case in his study. She thought they were beautiful.

When Marya was 15 years old, she graduated from high school with very high marks and was given a beautiful gold medal as a prize. Though her father was a respected teacher, the family was not rich. Marya had to find a job to get money for college.

She went to work as a governess, teaching and caring for the children of a wealthy family. But she still found time to read and study and to teach the children of poor families who lived nearby.

The years went by. Finally Marya was able to enter a great university, the Sorbonne, in Paris, France. When she registered for classes, she changed the spelling of her first name from the Polish Marya to the French Marie.

Though Marie was curious about everything, she soon found that science, especially chemistry, was her favorite subject. While she was still a student she met a brilliant young scientist named Pierre Curie. The two fell in love; when they were married she became Marie Curie.

A year later a new discovery attracted Marie Curie's curiosity. A French scientist, Henri Becquerel, discovered that the element uranium gave off mysterious, invisible rays of energy. Marie wanted to know if anything else also gave off these rays.

She began to experiment. After making tests on many different substances, she began to study pitchblende, a mineral that contains uranium and thorium. Marie discovered that thorium also gives off the rays.

After removing the small amount of uranium and thorium from the pitchblende, Marie was surprised and puzzled to find that the mineral remaining still gave off the mysterious rays.

What could cause such a thing? Marie wondered. At last she decided that the pitchblende must contain an even more active element—a new element!

Now Pierre Curie joined his wife in the search for the mystery element. Marie worked on separating the element from the pitchblende, while Pierre worked on studying the element itself and the rays it gave off.

Finally the Curies had collected a small sample of the pure element, which Marie called polonium, after her country Poland. She also gave a name to describe the release of the invisible rays of energy. She called the energy radioactivity.

But the Curies were amazed to find that the pitchblende contained yet another element—one that was even more radioactive!

Marie's curiosity drove her on. She wanted to collect a sample of the pure element, which she and Pierre named radium. It took four years, but from several tons of ore, Marie was able to get a tiny sample of the new element.

The Curies and Henri Becquerel in 1903 were given the Nobel Prize for their work on radioactivity. In 1911 Marie Curie was given a second Nobel Prize for her discovery of radium.

Marie Curie's curiosity had helped her to discover two new elements. Her curiosity about what radioactivity is brought about a new understanding of how atoms, the tiny building blocks of the universe, are put together. She was truly one of the world's great scientists.

Albert Schweitzer
and the Power of
Caring

ONE DAY, A FEW MONTHS AFTER his 21st birthday, Albert Schweitzer made a decision that was to change his entire life. He decided that after his 30th birthday he would spend the rest of his life helping human beings in some way. He did not know what kind of work he would do, but he had nine years to make up his mind.

Albert Schweitzer was born more than a hundred years ago in Alsace, which was then part of Germany but is now part of France. When he was five years old, he began to learn to play the piano. Three years later he started lessons on the organ; very soon he was good enough to play at church services.

When he was 18, Schweitzer went to the University of Strasbourg. The son of a minister, he was interested especially in theology, the study of religion. But when he was not studying or attending class, he would practice on the organ. His favorite composer was Johann Sebastian Bach, a famous German organist who lived about 300 years ago. While still a student, Schweitzer became an excellent musician and an expert on the life of Bach.

In those days in Germany, every young man had to spend a year training in the army. But even when the time came for Albert Schweitzer to take military training, he did not give up his studies. When he went on training exercises, he carried in his knapsack a copy of the Bible written in Greek, which he would study whenever he had spare time.

After Albert Schweitzer was graduated from the University of Strasbourg, he became a teacher and a preacher. He wrote a book about Bach and another book on the building and playing of organs. He also wrote two books on religion that are still read and discussed today.

But these successes were of little importance to Albert Schweitzer. In 1905, when he turned 30, he told his friends he wanted to be a doctor and open a hospital in Africa. He felt that caring for others when they became ill was a good way for him to spend his life.

It took courage to leave his comfortable home in Europe to go to Africa, but in 1913, Schweitzer, now a doctor, and his wife Hélène, traveled to Lambaréné, a village on the Ogowe River in what is now Gabon in west central Africa. There he built his hospital.

The hospital did not look like the hospitals in the United States. It was designed so that the path of the hot African sun would travel along the length of the roof to lessen the effects of the sun's heat. The roof also hung over the sides of the building, and this too helped block the sun's heat. Two sides of the building were made of mosquito netting. This kept the mosquitoes out while giving the hospital plenty of fresh, cool air. Later, houses were built around the hospital so the families of his patients could live in them while they helped care for their loved ones.

Soon people began to flock to Lambaréné to be healed by Dr. Schweitzer. They saw that he cared deeply about them, so the word spread and even more people came to

Lambaréné. Dr. Schweitzer worked very hard. He spent long hours in the operating room, visited all the patients at the hospital, and often worked far into the night. He seemed never to run out of energy.

When World War I broke out in 1914, Dr. Schweitzer had to close the hospital. Made a prisoner, he was sent back to Europe. But he never forgot the people he left behind. After the war ended, he returned to Lambaréné and rebuilt his hospital.

For nearly 40 years, Dr. Schweitzer continued his medical work in Africa. To help pay for his hospital he traveled to Europe to give organ concerts. He also gave the money he earned from his books to the hospital. Many people, after hearing Dr. Schweitzer talk about the hospital, gave money to help it grow and serve more people.

The story of Dr. Schweitzer has inspired many others to follow his example. One person, who started a hospital in Haiti, named it after Dr. Schweitzer; another person did the same thing in Peru.

Albert Schweitzer dedicated his life to helping others. His efforts made life better for thousands of people. He showed that caring about people should be an important part of all our lives.

Robert H. Goddard
and the Power of
Imagination

WHEN ROBERT H. GODDARD, America's pioneer rocket expert, was growing up in Massachusetts, he loved to study the things around him to see how they worked. His father did everything he could to help him learn. He gave him a telescope to look at the stars and planets and a microscope to study plant cells and bacteria. He even gave him a subscription to *Scientific American,* which told Robert about the latest discoveries of the world's great scientists.

Robert Goddard was born in 1882, more than 20 years before the Wright brothers flew their first airplane. Not a strong boy, he was often absent from school because of illness. But when he could not be in school, he would study on his own. The things Robert learned would wake up his imagination and give him ideas for experiments he wanted to try.

One time, using a thin sheet of aluminum, he tried to make a balloon. He filled it with hydrogen gas, but the balloon did not rise. The aluminum, of course, was too heavy.

Another time he tried to make diamonds by heating graphite, which is a form of carbon. This experiment also failed, but Robert was not discouraged. Even when his experiments did not work out as he hoped, he always learned something new and went on to try another experiment. His imagination never failed him.

Robert was especially interested in all kinds of flight. For example, he studied how birds fly and how they soar or change direction quickly. He also studied butterflies to learn how their wings work.

When he was 16 years old, he read a novel by H. G. Wells called *The War of the Worlds.* This story of Martians traveling millions of miles through space to Earth became one of his favorite books.

One October day, two weeks after his 17th birthday, Robert climbed an old cherry tree in his back yard in order to prune some of its branches. As he started to work, he began to wonder whether a machine could rise high from Earth and travel through space to other planets. He sat in the tree, looking far into the sky, and tried to imagine how the machine would work.

That day he told himself that he would devote his life to inventing a flying machine, a rocket-powered machine that would travel far from Earth into space.

From that time on, he was a very serious student. He learned everything he could about science and mathematics. Using his imagination and the things he learned, he began to experiment with rockets. After he became a professor of physics, he spent every minute of his spare time trying to make bigger and better rockets. Soon he became known as the man who wanted to fly to the moon.

Every time he launched a rocket, he learned something new. He was doing things no one had done before. In fact, he was inventing the science we call rocketry.

Goddard's rockets became ever bigger and more powerful. Realizing that a rocket would work best if it used liquid as the fuel, in 1926 he launched the first liquid-fueled rocket in history.

One test in 1929 was noisy enough to bring police and news reporters to Goddard's launch site. It was later reported that Goddard had tried to send a rocket to the moon but that it had crashed. Though Goddard explained that his rockets were small and could not fly beyond the test field, he was told not to launch any more of them in Massachusetts.

So in 1930 Robert Goddard looked for a new place to launch his rockets. He decided to move his laboratory to Roswell, New Mexico. There he set up shop and continued his experiments. His rockets flew higher and longer, helping him learn many things about the science of rocketry.

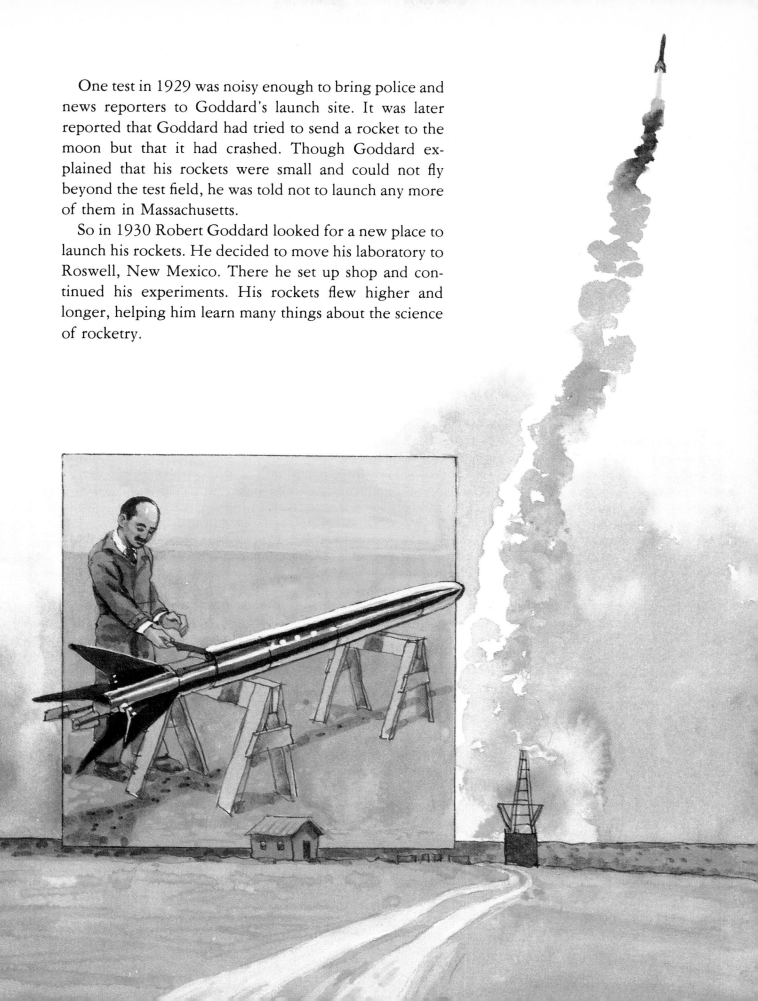

Others also learned from Goddard's experiments. His writings and patents were studied by rocket scientists in other countries. The German government in the 1930's, believing that rockets could be used as missiles in warfare, began to develop them. The first long-range missiles, the German V-2 rockets that struck England during World War II, were designed almost exactly like Goddard's rockets.

Robert H. Goddard received 214 patents for his inventions. He did not live to see the day when the first person walked on the moon, but he had learned enough to know that his dream of leaving Earth and traveling to the moon or Mars could become reality. It was Robert Goddard's imagination that showed us the way into space.

Will Rogers
and the Power of
Laughter

WILL ROGERS WAS BORN about a hundred years ago on his family's ranch near the city of Claremore, Oklahoma. In those days that part of Oklahoma was known as Indian Territory. It had been settled by Cherokee Indians, and Will's mother and father were part Cherokee Indian.

Will's father, a hard-working man, had one of the finest ranches in the territory. Many visitors stayed at the family's beautiful and roomy house. Here young Will met many interesting people.

When Will was very young, he learned to use a lasso. The rope was tied so that it formed a loop at the end. He would twirl the loop around and then snap the rope so the loop flew out and settled around a fence post or tree stump. When he pulled on the rope, the loop would tighten.

Soon he was catching, or "roping" as cowboys say, everything in sight, indoors and out. When he was five years old, he was given his first horse, and in no time he became an expert horseman. For young Will Rogers, happiness was a horse, a lasso, and the wide open range.

Then it came time for him to start school. He was never a good student. When he was older he was sorry he had not worked hard at getting a good education. He did not like to study. Instead he liked to tell jokes and stories, dazzle people with his rope tricks, and make people laugh.

Finally he left school and became a cowboy in Texas. For a while he worked as a cowboy in Argentina and South Africa.

Will Rogers liked being a cowboy, but his love of people and laughter led him finally to become an entertainer. The tricks he could do with the lasso got him jobs with shows in South Africa and Australia. Then he brought his act to New York City. Audiences liked his rope tricks and his wonderful way of telling jokes.

In a few years Will Rogers was appearing on Broadway, but his act had changed. He learned that people liked his sense of humor even more than his rope tricks. He talked about the events of the day, poking fun at just about everyone and everything in a gentle, good-natured way.

One time Will joked about doctors. "Personally, I have always felt that the best doctor in the world is the veterinarian. He can't ask his patients what is the matter—he's got to just know."

Another time he joked about one of his favorite subjects, politics and politicians. "I could study all my life and not think up half the amount of funny things they can think of in one session of Congress."

People everywhere came to know Will Rogers as the Cowboy Philosopher. His funny remarks often seemed to reveal some truth about life. Even as he made Americans laugh, he got them to think.

Once Will Rogers said, "I never met a man I didn't like." He never tried to hurt anyone for a laugh. He always treated laughter as a way to help people to understand one another better. He joked about presidents, politicians, and other important people, but very few became angry. In fact, almost everybody considered Will Rogers a friend.

When the Great Depression came, millions of people lost their jobs. Life was hard for nearly everyone. But Will Rogers helped cheer Americans. The laughter he brought into their lives gave them courage to forget their troubles and keep working for a happier future.

In 1935 Will Rogers was killed while flying in Alaska with his friend Wiley Post. People everywhere were sad about the loss of the man who had brought so much laughter into the world.

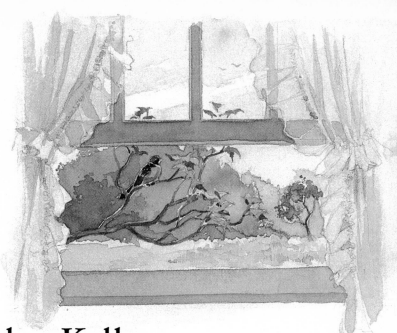

Helen Keller
and the Power of
Communication

IMAGINE A WORLD in which you could not see, hear, or speak. You would not enjoy music or marvel at the colors of a rainbow, or the dancing flight of a butterfly, or the sound of a waterfall. You would be unable to communicate, to talk to anyone or hear anyone when he or she spoke to you.

This was the world that a baby was plunged into during a winter more than a hundred years ago.

Helen Keller was born in Tuscumbia, Alabama. When she was nineteen months old, she became so ill that her parents worried that she would die. Helen somehow survived her terrible illness and grew stronger. But she had lost her eyesight and her hearing. For her, the world had become dark and silent.

As she grew older, Helen turned into a wild, moody child. If she did not get what she wanted, she would fly into a rage and end up sobbing bitterly.

She was a bright child. She had learned to make signs with her hands to show what she wanted. She was trying to communicate with others, but it was very hard to do.

Helen's parents had heard of a school in Boston, Massachusetts, called the Perkins Institute. Teachers there had helped another girl who was deaf and blind. The girl, Laura Bridgman, had even learned to read and write well enough to become a teacher at the institute. Helen's parents wrote to the headmaster of the school, who suggested that the Kellers hire Anne Sullivan to be Helen's teacher.

Miss Sullivan arrived in Tuscumbia when Helen was seven years old. Anne had been blind from childhood, but had regained some of her eyesight through a series of operations. A natural teacher, she was determined to succeed with Helen.

But the young girl first had to accept Anne Sullivan's authority. At first Helen resisted. One day she even locked Miss Sullivan in her room and hid the key. Helen's father had to put a ladder up to the window to get Miss Sullivan out of the room. Only months later did Helen return the key.

After a while, through firm but patient ways, Anne Sullivan gained Helen's confidence. She started to teach Helen the manual alphabet, in which each letter is represented by holding the fingers of the hand in a particular way. Day after day she would repeat the alphabet to Helen. Then she would touch Helen's hand to an object and spell out its name using the manual alphabet.

Though Helen repeated the hand motions, she did not yet understand that they spelled out the name of the object, and that every object had its own special name.

One day Miss Sullivan put Helen's hand under a stream of water pouring from a pump. In Helen's other hand she spelled out W-A-T-E-R.

Helen thought back to when she was a baby. Slowly she remembered that she had known a word for this cool, wet thing that poured onto her outstretched hand. What did it sound like? Wah-wah. W-A-T-E-R.

Water!

Suddenly Helen realized that her teacher was giving her the name for water, and in that moment she knew that everything had a name. Helen broke out into a big smile and excitedly repeated the letters to her teacher: W-A-T-E-R.

Now Anne Sullivan was filled with happiness. She had reached into Helen Keller's dark, silent world and had communicated with her. She had opened the door to a world of learning for Helen.

In the next few weeks Helen and her teacher shared the happiness of communicating. Helen learned hundreds of words, and soon she learned how to put together short sentences. By the end of the summer she was able to write a simple letter to her mother.

Over the years Anne Sullivan continued to be Helen's teacher, but there was much more to their relationship than that. The two became friends and companions. Helen Keller learned to read Braille, which is an alphabet for blind people. It uses patterns of raised dots to represent letters. Helen also learned how to speak, even though she could not hear herself.

When Helen Keller was 25 years old, she was graduated from Radcliffe College in Cambridge, Massachusetts, with honors. While she was a student at Radcliffe, a college for gifted young women, Helen wrote of her experiences in *The Story of My Life.* She dedicated her life to helping other people, especially the blind, and working for world peace. She wrote more books, including *Teacher,* a tribute to Anne Sullivan, the woman who gave her the gift of communication.

Eleanor Roosevelt
and the Power of
Service

IT IS EASY TO BELIEVE that rich children of important families are happier than other children, but Eleanor Roosevelt learned early in life that this is not always true.

She was born in New York City about a hundred years ago. Her parents were both members of old, well-established families. Her uncle was Theodore Roosevelt, who one day would become President of the United States.

But there was little happiness in Eleanor's young life. Her father Elliot Roosevelt suffered from alcoholism. As his drinking grew worse, family life became more and more unhappy. Finally, Eleanor's mother and father separated. When Eleanor was eight years old, her mother died and Eleanor went to live with her grandmother. Two years later, two months before Eleanor's tenth birthday, her father died.

Five years later Eleanor was sent to school in England. The headmistress of the school, Marie Souvestre, saw that Eleanor was a bright girl with hidden talents. She helped Eleanor learn that she had a quick mind and could be a good student. Eleanor also discovered she was looked up to as a leader by the other girls. Marie Souvestre and Eleanor became good friends. They went on

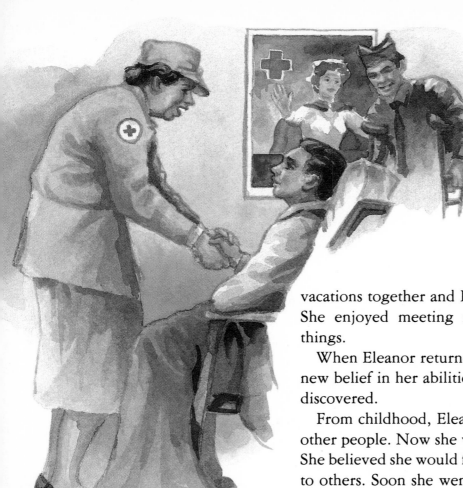

vacations together and Eleanor learned she liked travel. She enjoyed meeting new people and learning new things.

When Eleanor returned home she brought with her a new belief in her abilities and the new interests she had discovered.

From childhood, Eleanor had known the suffering of other people. Now she wanted to do something to help. She believed she would find happiness in being of service to others. Soon she went to work at a settlement house in a very poor section of New York City. A settlement house provides social services to poor people. For example, Eleanor taught dancing to the children who had no place else to go and gave them the chance to have fun. She was shocked to see the terrible conditions in which many people in big cities were forced to live.

When she was 24 years old, Eleanor Roosevelt was married to her distant cousin, Franklin Delano Roosevelt. Now she took on new responsibilities. She helped her husband as he worked his way through law school, cared for her mother-in-law, and began to raise a family.

Soon Franklin Roosevelt began his career in politics, and the family moved to Washington, D.C. When the United States entered World War I, Eleanor worked for the Red Cross, helping wounded soldiers who had returned from overseas.

Then tragedy struck once again. Her husband fell ill with polio, a crippling disease common in those days; he

lost the use of his legs. His mother wanted him to give up politics and live quietly at his family's home in Hyde Park, New York. But Eleanor supported Franklin's desire to go on with his career, encouraging him on his long struggle back to health and on his return to politics.

While Franklin was recovering his strength, Eleanor became more active in public affairs. She gave speeches, taught classes at a school for girls, became involved in business, and was soon accepted as an important member of the Democratic Party.

In 1928 Franklin Roosevelt was elected governor of New York. Four years later he was elected President of the United States. The Roosevelts returned to Washington and made the White House their home until Franklin Roosevelt's death in 1945.

At first Eleanor Roosevelt thought her position as First Lady would keep her from continuing her service to others. But she realized that she had been given a wonderful opportunity. Soon she was giving weekly press conferences, talking on the radio, and writing for the newspapers. Always, she urged citizens and public officials to do more to help those who needed help the most. It was not long before she became one of the most famous women in the world.

After Franklin Roosevelt's death, President Harry Truman asked Mrs. Roosevelt to serve as a delegate to the United Nations. She played a major role in writing the United Nations Declaration of Human Rights.

Eleanor Roosevelt worked for the benefit of humanity until her death. She showed how service to others is one of the best ways to have and to give happiness.

Mohandas K. Gandhi
and the Power of
Gentleness

ONE NIGHT IN 1893 a young lawyer from India named Mohandas K. Gandhi was traveling by train from Durban to Pretoria in South Africa. He was in South Africa to help an Indian merchant in a lawsuit. Once the young lawyer finished the case, he would go back to India. But something happened that would change his plans—and he would stay in South Africa for 20 years.

Gandhi had bought a first-class ticket, which meant that he could sit in a special place on the train. But soon a white passenger, accompanied by one or two railroad officials, came up to him. Gandhi was told that in South Africa only white passengers could travel first class. He would have to move back to the third-class railroad car.

"But I have a first-class ticket," Gandhi told them. "I always travel first class."

"That makes no difference. You must move to the third-class car or you will be thrown off the train."

"I will not move," Gandhi said.

When the train pulled into the next station, a policeman came onto the train and threw Gandhi and all his luggage off the train. The young lawyer spent the night

shivering in the cold railroad station. He had never been treated so unfairly in all his life.

After his experience on the train, Gandhi heard many stories about wrongs suffered by people from India who lived and worked in South Africa. He decided to stay for a while and do whatever he could to help them. He never dreamed that he would stay for 20 years. During that time he worked out his ideas about how to make things better for people and bring about change in the world.

Gandhi believed that when people see something wrong in the world, they should try to make it right. He said that gentleness, not violence, is the best way to make things better. People should refuse to accept injustice. They should protest, he said, by refusing to obey unjust laws. If that means they will have to go to jail, then they

should go to jail. They should meet other people's anger with love and understanding. They should try to turn those people into friends.

Gandhi went to prison many times because of his beliefs. His gentleness and courage turned many enemies into friends. A large number of people began to follow his way of protesting without using violence. As a result, over the years the Indians of South Africa succeeded in changing unjust laws and improving the condition of their lives.

In 1915 Gandhi finally returned to India, which was then part of the British empire. Soon, in the same way he had done in South Africa, he began to help the people. He showed how they could make their lives better by their own efforts, such as by making their own cloth for clothing and getting salt from seawater rather than buying it. Such self-help activities as these gave encouragement to the poor, who needed it most.

Gandhi also showed how the Indian people could win their independence from Great Britain without using violence. He said that the British rule of India was wrong. He said that if the people refused to support the government, the British would one day leave.

Many times Gandhi led peaceful demonstrations for independence. He would refuse to obey a law because he thought it was not right, and would go to prison for his refusal. Then others would refuse, and still more, until at last the law would be changed.

Sometimes Gandhi would stop eating in order to draw everyone's attention to a cause he believed in. Once he began a fast in support of mill workers who were thinking of giving up a strike they had begun. He told them he would not eat until they had won the strike. So the workers did not give up. In three days they reached an agreement with the mill owners to settle their differences, and the strike was settled.

Sometimes Gandhi fasted to end violence between Indians of the Hindu faith and those of the Muslim faith. Since neither the Hindus nor the Muslims wanted Gandhi to die because of their actions, they stopped fighting each other.

Because of the wisdom he showed in bringing about peaceful change, and the love he showed to all, he was called "Mahatma," which means Great Soul.

When India became independent in 1947, Mahatma Gandhi was honored as the father of his country. But he was not happy. India had been divided into a Hindu India and a Muslim Pakistan. In the confusion that followed, thousands were killed. Gandhi again fasted to end the violence between Hindus and Muslims. Many put away their weapons and promised not to use them again.

In 1948 Mahatma Gandhi was killed by a young Hindu who was angry about Gandhi's kindness toward Muslims. People in every country of the world mourned his death. Gandhi had shown the world the power of gentleness.

Jackie Robinson
and the Power of
Courage

IN THE SPRING OF 1947 a young man stepped up to home plate in a baseball game at Ebbetts Field in Brooklyn, New York, and made baseball history. His name was Jackie Robinson, and he was the first black person to play in major league baseball.

Jack Roosevelt Robinson was born in 1919 in Georgia, where his father and mother worked on a plantation. The family was very poor. When Jackie was still a baby, his father went looking for work in Texas. The family never heard from him again. His mother decided to move the family to Pasadena, California, to live with her brother.

When he was just a boy, Jackie found that some people were mean and cruel to him simply because he was black. Jackie's mother taught him that he was not to look for trouble, but always to have the courage to stand up for what he knew was right.

He was a good student, but it was sports that he liked most of all. He played hard and always tried his best to win. In high school he was a star on the football, basketball, baseball, and track teams. In college he set new records in all four of these sports, and also showed great talent for tennis and golf.

Jackie became a professional football player, but his football career ended in the same year it began, when the United States entered World War II. Soon he became a lieutenant in the United States Army. After the war he went back to professional sports, deciding this time to play baseball instead of football.

For many years black athletes had been kept out of major league baseball. The American and National leagues had only white baseball players, so black athletes played in their own leagues. Professional baseball had been run this way for so long that many people thought there was a law that no black player could play in the American or National leagues. But there was no such law.

Branch Rickey, president of the Brooklyn Dodgers, offered Jackie Robinson a contract to play for the Dodgers' minor league team, the Montreal Royals. Jackie knew that some people would be upset at the idea of blacks and whites playing baseball together. He would need great courage to face the taunts and insults that would come his way. He would have to keep his temper under control and play baseball better than ever.

Jackie also knew that his success would make it easier for other black athletes to play professional baseball but that, if he failed, it would be more difficult for them to become players in the major leagues.

He accepted Branch Rickey's offer. The next season, he dazzled fans and players with his hitting, fielding, and base-stealing. But his job required as much courage as he had expected. It was hard to shrug off the taunts and cruel remarks that people made, but he forced himself to do so. Sometimes he received threats of violence. Above all, he showed courage in refusing to give up.

Then Jackie Robinson joined the Brooklyn Dodgers. Again he faced the taunts of fans and players. There were times when he wanted to quit, but he always found the courage to keep going.

As the season went on, people began to see that he was a great baseball player. During his first year with the Dodgers he stole 29 bases, more than any other player in the National League, and he hit 12 home runs. His love of the game and desire to win seemed to inspire his teammates to greater efforts.

The Dodgers won the National League pennant and Jackie Robinson was named Rookie of the Year.

He showed that it takes courage to face difficult times and to right a wrong. Major league baseball was finally open to black athletes and Jackie Robinson was the man who led the way.

Glenn Cunningham
and the Power of
Determination

GLENN CUNNINGHAM WAS only a boy of eight when something happened that changed his life completely. His story is proof that sometimes determination, the ability to stick to a job until it is done, can turn the saddest story into a happy ending.

Glenn's family lived in Stevens County, Kansas, and early each school day Glenn and his older brother Floyd would hurry to the schoolhouse several miles from their home. On cold mornings it was their job to start a fire in the wood stove to warm up the schoolhouse before classes began.

In order to get the fire going quickly, they would sprinkle a little kerosene on the wood before lighting it. But one morning the liquid they used was gasoline. It had been put into the kerosene can by mistake. When they lighted the wood, there was a terrific explosion, and the little schoolhouse burst into flames.

Both Glenn and Floyd were very badly burned. Floyd died from his burns. For a time it seemed that Glenn would also die. But the brave eight year old fought the pain every minute and, after weeks of uncertainty, the doctors finally said he would live.

But, the doctors warned, they might have to take off both of Glenn's badly burned legs. To that Glenn said no, over and over. He was determined he would walk again.

Six months after the accident he was well enough to go outdoors on crutches to meet his friends. He wanted to show them how much better he was, but when he tried to stand without the crutches, he fell down. He had no feeling in his legs. It was as if he had no legs at all.

His friends were upset that Glenn could not walk, but he laughed bravely and said, "Never mind. Some day I will be able to walk. I'll even be able to run. And when I do, I'll outrun all of you!"

He set to work to make himself better. Every morning and night he rubbed his legs. All day he worked them to get some strength back into them. In a few months he was able to take a few clumsy steps. His family and friends were glad to see such progress in walking. But Glenn kept his real goal in mind all the time. He was determined to run again.

Within a couple of years Glenn Cunningham was running. For a long time it caused him great pain to walk, but running was painless. So everywhere he went, Glenn would run.

Four years after his accident, when he was only twelve years old, Glenn Cunningham ran in a race against high school runners—and beat them! Everyone at the race could see his courage and determination.

Glenn worked hard to gain every bit of strength and speed he could. He ate good foods, got plenty of sleep, and he ran, and ran, and ran. As a teenager, to build up his muscles, he took a job loading heavy bags of wheat. He won race after race in high school, where he set a new record of 4 minutes, 24.7 seconds for the mile run.

After that there was no stopping Glenn Cunningham. As a student at the University of Kansas, he won championships in the 800-meter and 1500-meter runs, and in 1933 he set a new U.S. and world record for the mile run of 4 minutes, 6.7 seconds.

At the 1936 Olympic Games, Glenn ran in the 1500-meter race and came in second, winning the silver medal. But he was very disappointed because he had wanted so much to win the gold medal. Still, he could not help noticing that the crowds cheered him as much as if he had won the gold medal.

And still he ran. Glenn became the greatest indoor mile runner of his day, winning an incredible number of races, including a total of 22 one-mile races at Madison Square Garden in New York City.

After he retired from running in 1940, Glenn Cunningham bought a ranch near Wichita, Kansas, and became a teacher. Though he and his wife raised twelve children, they still had plenty of time and room for youngsters who were in trouble and who needed a home where they could straighten out their lives. By the time of his death in 1988, Glenn Cunningham had helped about 9000 young people beat their problems and find their way in life.

A champion all his life, Glenn Cunningham proved to all of us that people can overcome great problems if they have enough determination.

Amelia Earhart
and the Power of
Adventure

EVEN AS A VERY YOUNG GIRL, Amelia Earhart loved adventure. Like all young people, she dreamed of doing exciting things with her life. But little did she know she would become one of the great fliers of all time.

She grew up in the early 1900's in Kansas, where she spent a happy and carefree childhood, dividing her time between her family's home in Kansas City and her grandparents' home in Atchison.

When Amelia was six years old, her father took the family to the St. Louis World's Fair. There Amelia and her little sister Muriel had great fun riding on the roller coaster.

At home Amelia got her uncle to help build her own roller coaster. The track ran down from the top of her father's tool shed. When it was finished Amelia was the first to try it. The cart made a terrible racket as Amelia went flying down the rickety track. Then the cart jumped the track and went flying into the air, dumping Amelia smack on the ground.

Amelia got up quickly and dusted herself off. She was excited by her adventure even though it did not turn out exactly the way she had planned it. She was about to try the ride again when her mother came out of the house to put an end to Amelia's experiments with her roller coaster.

Young Amelia Earhart especially liked sports and games. She enjoyed fishing with her father when he could spare time from his busy job as a railroad lawyer. In the summer she played football and went horseback riding and in the winter she liked sledding. One year she even talked her father into giving her a small rifle, which she used to shoot rats in the barn.

Amelia also liked to read. She spent many happy hours with books from her grandfather's library. Great novels and stories of adventure were all new experiences for Amelia.

When she was eleven years old, Amelia Earhart saw her first airplane, at the Iowa State Fair. She did not think much of it at the time. She was more interested in seeing the fair exhibits and going on the rides.

After graduating from high school in 1916, Amelia continued her education. But in the winter of 1917 her schooling was interrupted when she went to visit her sister, who was then attending school in Toronto, Canada. There Amelia saw soldiers who had been wounded in World War I, which had not yet ended. She decided to stay in Toronto and work as a nurse's aide. It was there that Amelia's interest in flying began. She spent many

hours watching the Canadian fliers practice loops and rolls and other flying exercises.

From that point on, Amelia Earhart worked to become a flier. In 1920 she made her first solo flight. She flew up into the sunlit sky, thrilled by the sense of freedom and adventure she felt in soaring a mile above Earth. When she landed she jumped out of the plane and said to her sister Muriel, "It's so breathtakingly beautiful up there! I want to fly whenever I can." And so she did. Over the next few years she continued to fly whenever she could.

In 1928 Amelia Earhart became the first woman to fly across the Atlantic Ocean, traveling from Newfoundland, in Canada, to Wales, in Great Britain, with fellow aviators Wilmer Stultz and Lou Gordon.

Almost instantly she became famous, and for the rest of her life she was able to do what she loved most—fly airplanes. She set new speed, distance, and altitude records. In 1932 she was the first woman to fly alone across the Atlantic Ocean, setting a new record time. In 1935 she became the first person to fly from Hawaii to the United States mainland. For her, each flight was a great new adventure.

In 1937 Amelia Earhart set out on her last adventure. With Fred Noonan as navigator, she left from Miami, Florida, on a round-the-world flight traveling eastward along the equator. On July 1 the pilots took off from New Guinea for Howland Island, a mere speck in the Pacific Ocean, more than 2500 miles away. They never reached the Howland airport. Although searchers made every effort to find them, not a trace of the brave fliers or their airplane was ever found.

Amelia Earhart was one of the last great pioneer aviators. She had shown that women were every bit as good as men when it came to flying. And she had shown that a person with a spirit of adventure can do great things.

Martin Luther King
and the Power of
Equality

ON THE FIRST DAY OF DECEMBER in 1955, Mrs. Rosa Parks stepped onto a bus in Montgomery, Alabama, and entered the pages of American history.

Mrs. Parks, a black woman, worked as a seamstress. That day she had worked hard and was very tired. After a short time the bus stopped and some white people got on. The bus driver told Mrs. Parks and some other black people that they had to move to the back of the bus so the white people could sit in front. According to a local law, Mrs. Parks had to give up her seat to a white passenger. Mrs. Parks refused to move. The bus driver called a policeman, who arrested Mrs. Parks.

For a long time the black citizens of Montgomery had suffered under a law that said blacks and whites could not sit together on public buses. The arrest of Mrs. Parks drew the blacks together. They decided to boycott the buses—they would not ride the buses until blacks were given the same rights as whites.

And who would lead the boycott? All agreed the job should go to Dr. Martin Luther King, Jr., pastor of the Dexter Avenue Baptist Church in Montgomery.

Dr. King knew that there were some blacks in Montgomery who thought that violence was the way to gain justice for black people. But Dr. King's hero was Mahatma Gandhi, who had shown that gentleness and love are much more powerful than violence and hatred. Dr. King told his followers that they should always act peacefully, no matter what happened.

The black citizens of Montgomery stopped riding the buses. They went to work and to the stores by sharing rides, by taking taxicabs run by other black citizens, and by walking.

The city officials tried to stop the boycott. Martin Luther King and many others were arrested, but the people refused to stop their boycott. Several times Dr. King received threats of violence.

One day someone threw a bomb onto the porch of Dr. King's house. No one was hurt in the explosion, but the crowd of people who gathered were angry that Dr. King and his family had been attacked. He spoke to them, saying that violence was not the way to gain justice. They must return hatred with love.

For a man whose house had just been bombed, it was a remarkable speech. Everyone went home, more convinced than ever that they had found a strong and brave leader.

The boycott lasted more than a year, but in the end the black citizens of Montgomery won the right to sit where they wanted on public buses. The boycott had succeeded.

The Montgomery bus boycott made Martin Luther King a hero to many people across America. He had shown that people could get justice through peaceful action.

Soon people in other cities were organizing to end other unjust laws. Dr. King traveled around the country, speaking to church groups and other gatherings about nonviolent change. He marched with protesters, who often included whites as well as blacks, and sometimes he was arrested with them.

Every year brought new gains for blacks. The nonviolent marches and demonstrations were often met with violence, but the people had taken Dr. King's message to heart. They refused to answer violence with more violence.

Year by year the movement to win equality for black people grew. In 1963 Martin Luther King was able to bring a quarter of a million Americans to Washington, D.C., to support new laws to guarantee civil rights for everyone. Dr. King spoke to the crowd, and his message was carried by radio and television to every city and town in the land and to nations around the world.

"I have a dream," he said, "that one day this nation will rise up and live out the true meaning of its creed: 'We hold these truths to be self-evident, that all men are created equal.'" In 1964 Dr. King was awarded the Nobel Peace Prize.

Dr. King was shot to death by an assassin on April 4, 1968, the victim of the violence he had fought against all his life. But his memory is still alive wherever people work peacefully for equality.

On January 20, 1986, Americans celebrated Martin Luther King Day, a new national holiday created to honor this great leader in the struggle for civil rights.

Mother Teresa
and the Power of
Compassion

COMPASSION OPENS OUR EYES and our hearts to the sorrow of others, and makes us want to help them.

About ten years ago, a small, thin woman dressed in a white *sari,* the traditional dress of the women of India, was given the Nobel Peace Prize. She was a Roman Catholic nun, known around the world as Mother Teresa. For more than 30 years, she had lived a life of poverty, devoted to serving the very poor around the world. The prize was recognition that her compassion for the neediest had taught us all to look beyond our own lives and help those who have nothing.

Mother Teresa was born in the city of Skopje, in Yugoslavia. Her full name was Agnes Gonxha Bojaxhiu. Her father was a successful merchant. Agnes lived with her parents and her older brother and sister in a large house surrounded by a beautiful garden. Her home was filled with love and happiness.

When Agnes was nine years old, her father died, leaving the family with practically nothing but their lovely home. To feed the family and pay the bills, Agnes's mother started her own business, selling cloth and carpets. She soon became very successful.

The Bojaxhius were a religious family, and they found strength and happiness in the teachings of their religion.

When Agnes was about twelve years old, she became convinced she was being called by God to be a missionary to serve the poor. Though she wanted to become a missionary, she did not want to leave her happy home and her friends.

But as the years went by, her belief that she was being called became stronger and stronger. When she was 18 years old, she said goodby to her family and friends. She joined a religious order called the Sisters of Loreto, who sent her to live and teach in Calcutta, India.

For many years Sister Teresa taught at St. Mary's High School in Calcutta. The boys and girls at the school lived in comfortable homes and had plenty to eat. They were not the poor children Sister Teresa had wanted to help, but she found great happiness in teaching them and serving as the school's principal.

Then, in 1946, while traveling from Calcutta to the city of Darjeeling, Sister Teresa was reminded of the terrible condition of the poor and hungry in India. Again she felt the call to serve the poorest of the poor. She realized she had to leave the lovely convent and school to live and work among the poor people of Calcutta.

Sister Teresa had to get special permission from the pope in Rome to make the move. Two years later she was given the permission she needed.

After three months of medical training, Sister Teresa went to live in the slums of Calcutta. There she found children living in the streets, dirty, hungry, and poorly clothed. She started a school for them, but because she had no place to use as a schoolhouse, the classes were held in the open air.

As more and more people found out about the work that Sister Teresa was doing, they offered help. Some gave money; others found a place for her school; and others, including some of her earlier students, joined her in her work.

Soon she had established a religious community called Missionaries of Charity. Sister Teresa became Mother Teresa.

In a few years Mother Teresa was given the use of two large rooms in a Hindu temple. There she brought poor people who were dying. She and the sisters fed and bathed them, offering them whatever loving care they could. Some who got well again began to work with Mother Teresa in helping other poor, sick people.

Mother Teresa established a special community where people suffering from the disease of leprosy could receive medical treatment and live decent lives. Since ancient times leprosy, which can leave people badly deformed or even kill them if it is untreated, has been a much feared disease, and lepers have been cast out and shunned. Mother Teresa, full of compassion for these most miserable of the poor, found them a place where they could live comfortably.

Every year more women became sisters of the Missionaries of Charity. As the religious community began to grow, it sent sisters to live and work among the poor and sick in other cities in India, and finally in cities around the world.

Mother Teresa's example has made many others dedicate their lives as she dedicated hers. They continue to carry her message of compassion and love to the poor around the world.

America's Story

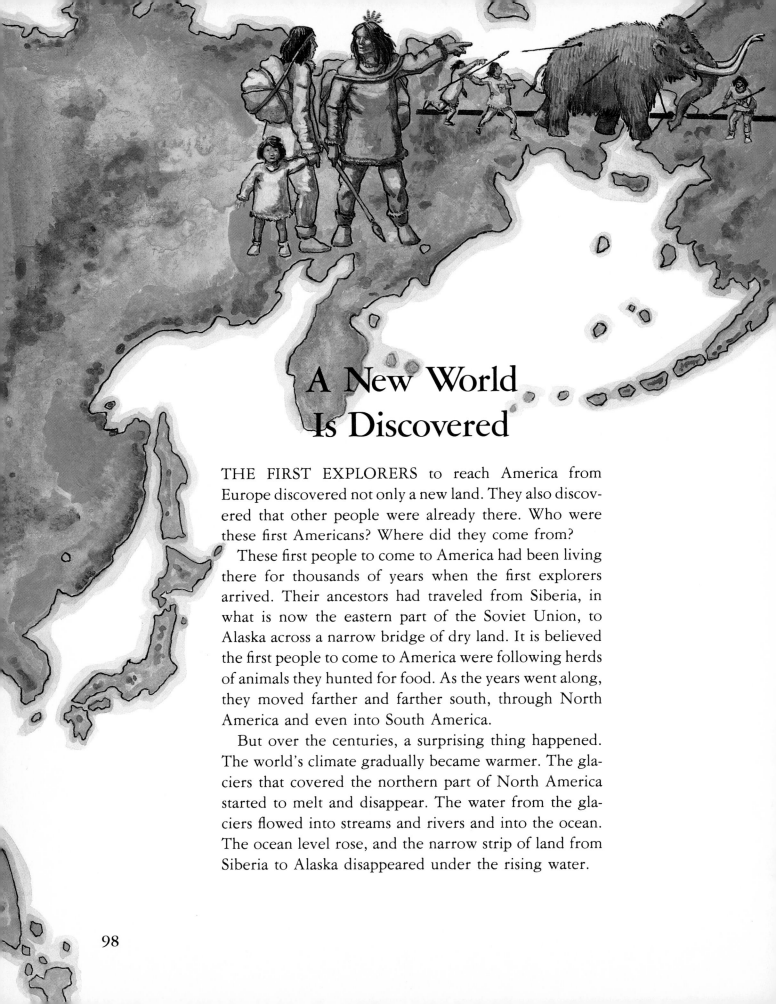

A New World
Is Discovered

THE FIRST EXPLORERS to reach America from Europe discovered not only a new land. They also discovered that other people were already there. Who were these first Americans? Where did they come from?

These first people to come to America had been living there for thousands of years when the first explorers arrived. Their ancestors had traveled from Siberia, in what is now the eastern part of the Soviet Union, to Alaska across a narrow bridge of dry land. It is believed the first people to come to America were following herds of animals they hunted for food. As the years went along, they moved farther and farther south, through North America and even into South America.

But over the centuries, a surprising thing happened. The world's climate gradually became warmer. The glaciers that covered the northern part of North America started to melt and disappear. The water from the glaciers flowed into streams and rivers and into the ocean. The ocean level rose, and the narrow strip of land from Siberia to Alaska disappeared under the rising water.

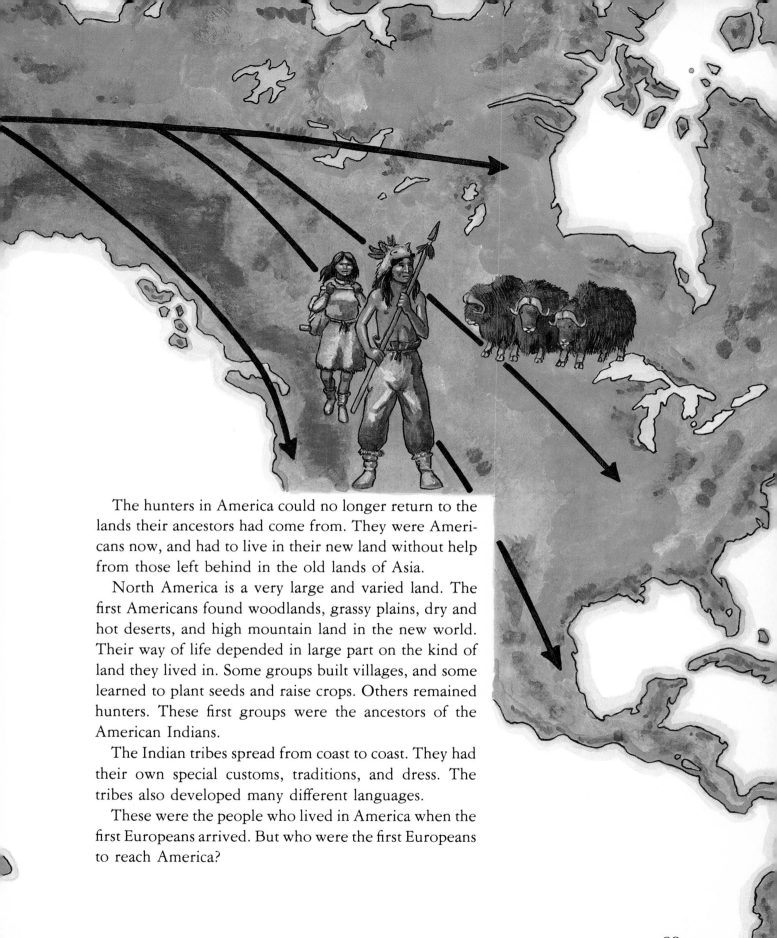

The hunters in America could no longer return to the lands their ancestors had come from. They were Americans now, and had to live in their new land without help from those left behind in the old lands of Asia.

North America is a very large and varied land. The first Americans found woodlands, grassy plains, dry and hot deserts, and high mountain land in the new world. Their way of life depended in large part on the kind of land they lived in. Some groups built villages, and some learned to plant seeds and raise crops. Others remained hunters. These first groups were the ancestors of the American Indians.

The Indian tribes spread from coast to coast. They had their own special customs, traditions, and dress. The tribes also developed many different languages.

These were the people who lived in America when the first Europeans arrived. But who were the first Europeans to reach America?

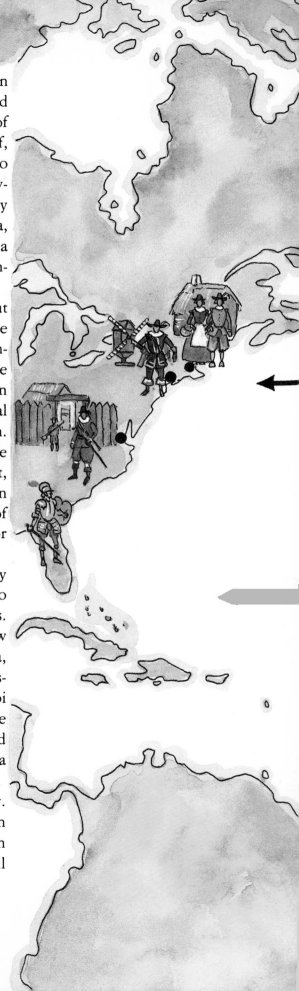

Many people believe that Leif Ericsson, a sea captain from Norway, was the first. Leif's father, who was called Eric the Red, had already sailed to the Arctic island of Greenland and had established a small colony there. Leif, who came to be known as Leif the Lucky, set out to explore the world farther west of Greenland. He discovered a new land which he called Vinland. Today, many people believe he first landed on the Labrador peninsula, in what is now eastern Canada, and later established a small settlement in northern Newfoundland, on Canada's eastern coast.

Christopher Columbus, who was born in Italy but sailed under the Spanish flag, is the best known of the early explorers. Columbus never set foot on the mainland of North America. But in the four voyages he made between 1492 and 1504, he discovered many islands in the Caribbean Sea and landed on the coasts of Central and South America. All these lands he claimed for Spain.

The English were also among the first to sail across the Atlantic Ocean and explore the New World. John Cabot, an Italian who lived in England, discovered Cape Breton Island—the easternmost part of the Canadian province of Nova Scotia—and Newfoundland, and claimed both for England.

In the 1500's the New World began to attract many explorers and adventurers, some of them hoping to become rich by finding vast treasures of gold and jewels. The Spanish were very active in exploring the New World. Ponce de León discovered and named Florida, and Hernando de Soto explored parts of Georgia, Mississippi, and Louisiana, and discovered the great Mississippi River. Francisco Vasquez de Coronado explored the plains of Texas and Kansas and discovered the Grand Canyon. Spain claimed all of this land, calling it Nueva España, or New Spain.

Far to the north the English explorers were also busy. Henry Hudson sailed up the Hudson River as far north as present-day Albany; he also discovered Hudson Bay in Canada. Sir Francis Drake, the first Englishman to sail

around the world, stopped in California and claimed it for England.

French explorers also explored North America. Jacques Cartier discovered and explored the St. Lawrence River. Samuel de Champlain discovered Lake Champlain in New York and also Lake Huron, one of the five Great Lakes located between the United States and Canada.

These explorers from different countries all helped to explore America, but where did the name America come from? It came from one of the first explorers, Amerigo Vespucci, an Italian who sailed for Spain. He wrote an account of his voyage, and in 1507 a German mapmaker named the New World "America" in honor of him.

101

The Problems
of the First Colonies

THE EARLY EXPLORERS OF AMERICA returned to Europe with exciting stories of the new land they had found. According to these tales, America was so big that anyone who wanted to have his own farm could do so, and the soil was so rich that the crops would grow almost by themselves. The waters off the American coast were full of fish. Vast stretches of woodland promised an almost endless supply of lumber, and a person could become rich by trading with the Indians for valuable beaver furs.

These descriptions of America helped draw settlers from Europe to the new land. Some of these settlers came to get away from the almost constant wars that were being fought in Europe. Others came to start up their own farms or businesses, or simply to find work. Still others came to America so they could practice their religious beliefs freely and without fear.

In a way, many of the first colonists came to America in order to get away from the problems facing them in Europe. Yet once they got to America, they found that this land of great promise presented them with a whole new set of problems.

In England, the man most determined to colonize the new land was Sir Walter Raleigh, who was a favorite of Queen Elizabeth I. Raleigh organized an expedition in 1584 to explore the coast of North America. When the explorers returned to England, they told Raleigh they had found a rich and wonderful land that was perfect for settlement. Raleigh was overjoyed with this success. He called the new land Virginia.

Sir Walter Raleigh was able to persuade the queen to finance a new expedition to set up a colony in the New World. However, much to his disappointment, the queen would not permit him to go with the colonists. She insisted he remain in England at the royal court.

The first major expedition—over 600 men—left England for America in April of 1585. Three months later it reached the island of Roanoke, just off the coast of what is now North Carolina. About 100 men stayed at the Roanoke settlement when the ships returned to England for supplies.

The settlers were soon beset by trouble. The supply ships did not return on schedule, and food became scarce. The Indians, who at first had been friendly, turned against the settlers and refused to help them or give them any food.

The next summer Sir Francis Drake, who had been given permission by the queen of England to attack Spanish ships and colonies in the New World, stopped by the island. The discouraged settlers decided to abandon the colony and ship back to England with him.

Sir Walter Raleigh was disappointed that the colony had been abandoned, but he was determined to establish a permanent colony at Roanoke. A second expedition, this time including men, women, and children, reached the island late in July of 1587.

The next month, on August 18, a baby girl was born to Eleanor White Dare, the daughter of the colony's leader. She was the first English child born in America. She was given the name Virginia Dare. A few days later, a second child was born at Roanoke.

When the ships that had brought the colonists to Roanoke sailed away, they left 116 people—88 men, 17 women, and 11 children. But when the English ships returned in 1590, there was no trace of the Roanoke colonists. Their homes were deserted.

Roanoke became known as the Lost Colony.

No one knows what happened to the Roanoke settlers. It may be that hunger forced them to move and to look for a village of friendly Indians who would feed them, but no one can say for certain.

In 1607 a new attempt was made to plant an English colony in the New World. A group of merchants in London sent an expedition to Jamestown, in Virginia. Jamestown had its problems, too. Many of the men who came over from England preferred searching for gold to planting needed crops or building secure homes. As a result, many of the colonists died of disease and starvation in the first year.

But an able leader rose in Jamestown and helped the colony survive that first bitter winter. He was Captain John Smith, a brave, strong man who had been a soldier for many years.

Smith was a member of the council that governed the tiny colony. In the fall of 1607 Smith left to bargain for food from the Indians. During his travels he became injured and was captured by unfriendly Indians. The Indian chief, Powhatan, ordered Smith to be put to death. But according to Smith's own account, he was rescued at the last moment by Powhatan's daughter, the Indian princess Pocahontas. Pocahontas had nursed the injured Smith back to health. Now she was able to talk her father into letting Smith live.

Powhatan and his tribe then became good and true friends of the Jamestown colonists.

Smith returned to Jamestown just as supplies arrived from England. He was elected leader of the colony in the fall of 1608. Smith governed wisely but with a firm hand. The colony survived, and Smith returned to England in 1609.

After a time Pocahontas became a Christian and took the name Rebecca. In 1614 she married the English settler John Rolfe. They sailed to London in 1616. One year later Pocahontas was dead, a victim of smallpox. Her son, Thomas, was educated in England. He returned to America and became an important person in Virginia. Many of his descendants live there today.

Roanoke was not a successful colony, but it set the stage for Jamestown, the first permanent English settlement in America.

The Pilgrims Sail
for America

THE STORY OF THE PILGRIMS in America really begins in England in 1606. At that time a group of people called Separatists lived in England. They were called Separatists because they had separated from the official Church of England and had formed their own religious group. Later they would be called Pilgrims. A pilgrim is a person who travels to a place that is sacred to his or her religion. A pilgrim can also be any traveler or wanderer to a distant place.

King James I of England had ruled that everyone should worship in the Church of England, but the Separatists were determined to worship God according to their own beliefs. They met secretly in each other's homes. When King James learned of this, he became very angry. Separatist leaders were arrested and put in jail. Although no Englishman was permitted to leave England without the king's permission, the Separatists found ways to leave quietly in small groups. They sailed to Holland where they could have religious freedom.

For eleven years the Separatists lived in Holland. When they heard that Spain, a Catholic nation, might be

planning to interfere with the freedoms they had found in Holland, they decided once again to leave. William Brewster, one of their leaders, suggested that they journey to America.

English businessmen provided the money needed for the expedition after the Separatists promised to send furs and lumber to them from America. Some of the Separatists decided not to go, but the businessmen found 70 other people who wanted to work in America. They hired a ship, the *Mayflower,* and the Separatists joined them in England aboard their own ship, the *Speedwell.* The *Speedwell* was much smaller than the *Mayflower.*

Twice the expedition set sail for America, and each time the *Speedwell* developed leaks and forced the expedition to turn back. Finally the leaders of the expedition decided to leave the little *Speedwell* behind. It was just not sturdy enough for the long voyage to America.

On September 6, 1620, more than one hundred passengers crowded aboard the *Mayflower* and set out for America from Southampton, England. Captain Christopher Jones commanded the ship. Another member of the expedition was red-haired Miles Standish, a soldier chosen by the organizers of the expedition to command the colonists' defenses. Standish had a fiery temper to match his red hair. He had insisted that guns and gunpowder be brought along for protection against unfriendly Indians they might find in America.

In early November, after a long voyage across the Atlantic Ocean, the weary passengers heard the welcome cry of "land ahoy!" They had reached Cape Cod, a long arm of land stretching out from the coast of New England. The settlers had been given permission to settle in Virginia, but storms had blown them far off course.

The Pilgrim leaders knew that the charter they had been given in England was legal only in Virginia. They decided to write up a new plan for governing their colony. This new plan, called the Mayflower Compact, stated that the colonists would elect their own leaders and vote on the laws that would govern them. The Mayflower Compact was the first democratic document in the New World.

Captain Jones told the colonists that English fishermen had been to this part of America, but no English people had tried to live there. There would be no one to prevent them from settling there if they wanted to.

"Except for the Indians," Miles Standish reminded them. He said that he would go ashore first with a small group of men to make sure it was safe. When he returned he brought both good and bad news. They had seen the Indians, who appeared to be friendly, but they had been unable to find any fresh water. All the ponds and inlets were salty seawater. No colony could be established without plenty of fresh water.

Standish made another trip farther along the coast of the cape. This time he reached Plymouth harbor. There was fresh water nearby, and the land looked excellent for farming. Soon the *Mayflower* sailed into Plymouth harbor and dropped anchor.

On the day after Christmas, 1620, the first colonists left the *Mayflower* and went ashore to their new home in America.

The Pilgrims' first winter in the New World was a hard one. More than 40 of the settlers died of disease.

In the spring a friendly Indian named Samoset visited the settlers. "Welcome," he said. The Pilgrims were amazed to be greeted in their own language by an Indian. Samoset explained to them that English fishermen had taught him how to speak English.

About two weeks later, Samoset brought an Indian friend named Squanto to visit the Pilgrims at their new

settlement. Squanto also spoke English. Years earlier he had been taken to England by some fishermen. After living in England for several years, Squanto had returned to America only to find that all the members of his tribe had died from disease. The Pilgrims had settled on the land where his people once had lived.

Squanto decided to live with the settlers. He showed them the best places to hunt and to catch fish. He showed them how to place a fish in the ground along with a few kernels of corn. That way the corn plants would grow tall and strong and produce rich, tasty ears of corn. Squanto also showed them how to plant other crops, such as beans and pumpkins.

Squanto also acted as the Pilgrims' guide and interpreter. He helped the Pilgrims arrange a peace treaty with the Wampanoag Indians, who lived in the area around Plymouth colony. The chief of the Wampanoags, Massasoit, was a true friend to the Plymouth colonists. During Massasoit's long life, the Wampanoags remained at peace with the newcomers to America.

The Pilgrims' first harvest was bountiful. Their governor, William Bradford, said that it was time to give thanks to God for the good things that had come to them. They invited their Indian friends to the feast. Thus, the Pilgrims began the custom of Thanksgiving.

New Amsterdam Becomes New York

THE INDIANS WERE THE ORIGINAL settlers of the area now called New York City. They named their favorite island Ma-na-hat-ta, which means Heavenly Land. Years later it would be known as Manhattan Island.

European explorers knew of the island. They had sailed along the coast and sometimes had sailed into what is now known as New York Harbor. But none of the early explorers had actually set foot on the land until the arrival of Henry Hudson, an English explorer who sailed for the Dutch.

In 1609 the Dutch East India Company hired Henry Hudson to find a shorter way to reach the Orient. Hudson had already made two unsuccessful attempts to sail northeast around Europe to the Orient. This time, however, he decided to go west. Crossing the Atlantic Ocean, Hudson arrived off the coast of North America. He sailed his little ship, the *Half-Moon,* into the waters of the fine harbor and sent some of his crew ashore to explore the island the Indians called Ma-na-hat-ta. Then Hudson sailed the *Half-Moon* up the river that came to bear his name. Hudson did not discover a water route to the

Orient, but his voyage gave the Dutch their claim to this region of the New World.

The Dutch built a trading post on the island Hudson's men had explored. Colonists soon followed and settlement of the Dutch colony of New Netherland began. In 1625 four Dutch ships arrived. They were named the *Cow,* the *Pig,* the *Sheep,* and the *Horse,* after the cargoes they carried. The Indians watched with amazement as the animals were unloaded, for they had never seen such creatures before.

The next year Peter Minuit was appointed to serve as governor of the colony. He decided to buy the island of Ma-na-hat-ta from the Indians. He offered the Indian leaders a collection of such items as tools, knives, axes, cloth, and beads. These things were worth about 60 guilders. A guilder was the Dutch unit of money and was a full day's pay for the average Dutch laborer.

The Indians accepted Peter Minuit's offer because the tools were far better than any they had ever seen. Also, they could not understand how anyone could own the land. To their way of thinking, people belonged to the land, not the other way around.

This was how Ma-na-hat-ta island became Dutch property. The happy Dutch settlers named their island settlement New Amsterdam.

About 20 years later, Peter Stuyvesant arrived as governor. Stuyvesant was an old soldier who had lost his leg in battle. He stomped around the settlement on his wooden leg decorated with silver bands. What he saw was an untidy village of about 700 people. Cows, pigs, chickens, and geese roamed in the streets. Rubbish was everywhere. Stuyvesant took command right away. He ordered the rubbish carted away and the animals fenced in.

Stuyvesant was a strict governor. He was not very popular, mostly because he made the people pay taxes and enacted laws they did not like. The people of New Amsterdam had many nicknames for Peter Stuyvesant—including "Old Silver Nails," perhaps because of the silver nails in his wooden leg.

But Peter Stuyvesant earned the people's respect, for all could see that New Amsterdam had grown into a prosperous and peaceful Dutch town, the finest settlement in the entire Dutch colony of New Netherland.

Things were not to remain peaceful, however.

The English also claimed the area because it had been explored by John and Sebastian Cabot, father and son, whom the English had hired to sail for them. But for a long time the English did little to challenge the Dutch claim in the New World. They were too busy with their European wars.

Gradually, though, the English had begun to dislike the idea of a thriving Dutch colony between the English colonies of Plymouth and Jamestown.

In 1664 four English ships dropped anchor in the harbor and trained their guns on New Amsterdam. The English commander ordered Stuyvesant to surrender the colony. "Never will I surrender," Stuyvesant replied. The townspeople realized that they were untrained to fight the heavily armed soldiers and their deadly cannons. Finally, they forced a heartbroken Stuyvesant to surrender.

King Charles II of England gave the colony to his brother James, duke of York and Albany, and the town of New Amsterdam was renamed New York.

For a brief time in 1673 the Dutch regained control of their beloved New Amsterdam, but their good fortune was short-lived. In Europe Holland lost a war with England. The peace treaty that was signed officially gave New Netherland to England. The colony was renamed New York. A new charter, which guaranteed to the Dutch settlers the rights of freedom of worship and trial by jury, was given to the local officials.

English rule had begun, but the Dutch had planted their colorful history and traditions in the New World. The Dutch continued to play an important part in the growing English colony of New York.

The French and Indian War

BETWEEN 1689 AND 1763 Great Britain and France fought four great wars. The two countries fought against each other both in Europe and in America. In each war, French troops and their Indian allies attacked the English colonies. In return, British troops and their Indian allies raided French forts and settlements.

During the first three of these wars there were many bloody battles. But the treaties that ended each war left the British and French colonies almost exactly the way they were before the fighting broke out.

The fourth and most important struggle between the French and British began in 1754. The war in America was known as the French and Indian War. It was a battle for the rich lands drained by the Ohio River, between the Appalachian Mountains and the Mississippi River. Both countries claimed this land.

France and England had gone about colonizing the new land in different ways. Both countries had tried to make friends with the Indians, but the French had built forts and established trading posts, while the English colonists had built towns and settlements.

When war came, the many scattered settlements of the English proved more difficult to defend than the few forts and trading posts of the French. As the French won skirmish after skirmish, more and more Indian tribes joined them, eager to be on the winning side.

The worried British sent one of their best generals to command the British forces in America. He was Edward Braddock, a brave military man who fought by the rulebook as he had been taught in Europe. Braddock's plan was to capture Fort Duquesne, a French stronghold located where the city of Pittsburgh, Pennsylvania, now stands. With a force of 1200 men, including a young colonial officer from Virginia named George Washington, Braddock started forth. Ignoring the advice of Washington and friendly Indian guides on the best way to fight in the wilderness, Braddock marched his red-coated troops in straight and orderly military columns. Along the way they built a road through the wilderness.

As the British neared Fort Duquesne, they were met by the French and their Indian allies. The French and Indians kept themselves well concealed behind trees, rocks, and fallen logs. The British and Americans fought in the open. Braddock's troops could not see their

enemies, but they were perfect targets for the French and Indians. Braddock, three-fourths of his officers, and over half of his troops were killed. George Washington led those who were left to safety.

This bloody defeat was an important lesson for the British. New officers trained in wilderness fighting and more skilled British and colonial troops eventually turned the tide of the war in favor of the British.

The final battle was fought on the Plains of Abraham, a large flat area, or plateau, outside the city of Quebec in Canada. General James Wolfe led a British army in an attempt to capture Quebec. He took his men up the St. Lawrence River above the city. Then, at night, he moved his troops to positions on a steep bluff known as the Heights of Abraham.

When the French commander, Louis Montcalm, discovered the British troops the next morning, he decided to fight them where they were. Montcalm and his forces stopped the first English attempt to take the city, but the French could not withstand the heavy fire from the English. Eventually they retreated in disorder. Both commanders were killed in the battle. A few days later the city of Quebec surrendered to the British, and soon all of Canada was under British control.

The French and Indian War was ended in 1763 by the Treaty of Paris. This treaty gave the British all of Canada and all of the French possessions east of the Mississippi River. France had lost its once great North American empire.

The struggle between England and France for colonial possessions in North America was over. In towns and villages throughout the English colonies, people cheered the British soldiers and toasted King George III, who had become the king of England three years earlier. The American colonists were looking forward to peace and prosperity.

Tea, Taxes, and War Clouds

THE ENGLISH COLONISTS in America had rejoiced when the long series of wars between Great Britain and France ended with a British victory. They were looking forward to living in peace, settling the new-won land, and building up their businesses and trade. But there was trouble ahead for the colonists.

Wars cost money, and the cost of winning a war continues even after the shooting has stopped. Great Britain had won new territories. This meant it had new responsibilities. Troops had to stand watch on the frontier. Settlements had to be built in the new territories. These things cost money.

The citizens of England were already heavily taxed, and so the British Parliament and King George III decided that the American colonists should be taxed as well. After all, the colonists had the most to gain from the new frontier that had been won. It seemed only fair to the king and to his advisers that the colonists help pay the cost of winning it.

The year 1764 marked the beginning of the program to tax the colonies. The British government thought of

a number of new taxes. A tax was placed on sugar brought into the colonies. The Stamp Act stated that all newspapers and legal documents would have to carry a special stamp purchased from the British government.

The colonists were very angry. They objected to the taxes. They also thought it unfair that they were not allowed to send anyone to the British Parliament to represent them.

British officials in the American colonies found it difficult to collect the taxes from the outraged citizens. At last the Stamp Act was repealed and the sugar tax was reduced.

Then new taxes were passed on tea and other items shipped into the colonies. Again there was a great outcry. The saying, "No taxation without representation," was heard throughout the colonies. In every colony groups of citizens protested the unjust taxes. Once again the British backed down. All the new taxes were repealed except the one on tea.

This was not enough for many colonists and they continued their protests. In the port city of Boston, British officials who tried to collect taxes were tarred and feathered.

An angry King George III sent his scarlet-coated soldiers to uphold law and order. "Lobster backs!" the people shouted at the soldiers. "Redcoats!"

On a snowy March night in 1770, an angry confrontation between a group of British soldiers and the citizens of Boston led to tragedy. The soldiers were insulted and pelted with snowballs by a group of young Bostonians. Suddenly, gunshots rang out. The soldiers fired into the crowd and five people were killed. In America this sad event was called the Boston Massacre. Americans became more and more determined that there should be no British armies on American soil.

Other clashes between the British authorities and the American colonists followed. Just south of Providence, Rhode Island, an English customs ship ran aground. Eight boatloads of men left Providence, attacked the ship, and burned it. The king ordered that those responsible should be brought to justice. In all of Providence, however, the British could not find a single person who would identify the men. Eventually the case was dropped.

Did you ever hear of anyone getting so angry that he had a party? This is exactly what happened in 1773. That year the British Parliament passed the Tea Act, which gave the British East India Company the right to sell tea at a low price in America. Many colonial merchants had already bought tea at higher prices. Their businesses would be ruined.

This was too much for the unhappy colonists. It was time to strike and the Americans made ready. When the ship *Dartmouth,* the first of three ships carrying tea to Boston, sailed into the harbor, the citizens tried every lawful means they could think of to get the tea sent back to England. They were determined not to let the tea get into Massachusetts. But all their efforts failed.

Finally, a group of patriots decided it was time for a "party" they had planned as a last resort. On the evening of December 16, 1773, a group of citizens gathered in a final attempt to get the tea shipped back to England.

When it failed, about 50 men disguised as Mohawk Indians gave a wild war whoop and rushed to the wharf
where the three tea ships were anchored. The raiders,
wearing burnt cork on their faces and carrying hatchets,
boarded the ships. One by one, all 342 tea chests on
board the ships were smashed open and their contents
dumped into the harbor. Nothing else was damaged. No
one was hurt.

Soon throughout America colonists were talking about
the Boston Tea Party.

When King George heard about the Boston Tea Party,
he was enraged. At his urging, Parliament called for stiff
measures to punish the rebellious citizens of Boston.
Ships were forbidden to load or unload cargoes in the
Port of Boston. Members of the Massachusetts House of
Representatives and other government officials were no
longer to be chosen by the colonists, but by the king. A
law called the Quartering Act required that the colonists
provide room in their own homes for British soldiers.

The American colonists began to realize that they must
unite to protect their freedom. There was even talk of
war against mighty England.

The Shot Heard Round the World

IN SEPTEMBER OF 1774, patriot leaders from the American colonies gathered in Philadelphia to discuss ways to get the British government to stop mistreating the colonies. Most of the delegates were shocked to learn that the men from Boston wanted complete freedom from England. The majority decided that the best action was to write a letter to King George III, asking that the colonists be treated with the same rights and justice as other Englishmen. The letter was written and sent to the king, but the colonists received no reply.

Talk of rebellion increased. In Massachusetts, the farmers began training for war. They called themselves Minutemen because they were ready to fight at a minute's notice.

In March of 1775, Patrick Henry spoke at a meeting in Virginia. "We must fight! I repeat it, sir, we must fight!" he said. "I know not what course others may take, but as for me, give me liberty or give me death." More and more people were beginning to agree with his belief that the colonies would have to fight for their rights.

The Minutemen of Massachusetts added to their store of gunpowder and bullets hidden away in the village of Concord. In Virginia, plantation owners started training companies of soldiers. George Washington was asked to command the Virginia troops, and he agreed to do so.

Then one day, a 13-year-old boy in Boston who was holding horses for some British officers overheard an alarming conversation. The soldiers spoke of a plan to seize the military supplies that were stored in Concord. Some loyalists who thought that the colony should remain true to King George III had informed them about the hidden supplies.

The boy went to some citizens who supported the patriot cause and told them about the conversation he had overheard. They sent him to Paul Revere's home with the news. Revere had promised to get word to Concord if the British marched forth from Boston.

The patriots of Boston were watching the British troops carefully. It had been arranged that, at the first sign the troops were heading for Concord, a signal would be flashed by lantern from the tower of the North Church—one lantern if the soldiers were marching by a longer land route, and two lanterns if they were taking the shorter route and crossing the Charles River by boat.

On the night of April 18, Paul Revere was watching the church tower when he saw the signal he had been waiting for. Two lanterns—the Redcoats were crossing by boat. He jumped on his horse and raced out along the road leading to the villages of Lexington and Concord, warning every farmhouse along the way that the British were coming. Another man, William Dawes, also rode out to warn the Minutemen. Paul Revere was captured just after he rode through Lexington, but Dawes was able to get to Concord and warn the Minutemen there.

When the British arrived at Lexington in the early dawn, a ragged line of Minutemen waited for them on the town green. The British officers were furious. Law and order were being defied. The leader of the British advance party was Major John Pitcairn. "Lay down your arms and go back home," he ordered the single line of Minutemen. After a while the patriots began to move off the green but they did not lay down their muskets.

Then someone fired a shot. No one was ever certain from which side the first shot came, but it became known as the "shot heard round the world."

The fight lasted less than half an hour. Short of ammunition but long on courage, the Minutemen stood their ground as long as they could. Eight Americans lost their lives and ten were wounded. Only one British soldier was hurt.

The British, rejoicing in their easy victory, set out for Concord. By the time they reached the town, most of the military supplies had been carried away. About 400 Minutemen had gathered on high ground overlooking the Concord bridge. As they watched the British searching their homes, the patriots decided to march back into the village. With a drummer and fifer at the head of their column, they advanced toward the bridge. The British tried ripping up the bridge planks, then fired their muskets at the advancing Americans. Still the colonists marched forward. "Fire," shouted one of the American officers. The first American volley killed three British soldiers and wounded many others.

The British troops marched back to Boston that afternoon, but at every turn in the road, from behind trees and stone walls, patriot marksmen fired deadly volleys at them. Many British soldiers were killed that afternoon. To the British, it seemed as if the whole countryside had taken up arms against them.

Back in Boston, the British commander organized his troops and fortified the city. The American Revolution had begun.

American Patriots and the Declaration of Independence

AFTER THE BATTLES of Lexington and Concord, the American patriots found themselves at war with Great Britain. Some of the patriot leaders hoped that the break between the British government and the American colonies could be mended, but as the war went on, more and more colonial leaders became convinced that peace would come only with American independence.

Who were the American patriots who risked their lives by openly challenging the authority of the British king and Parliament?

Three of the best-known patriot leaders came from Massachusetts. They were Samuel Adams, John Adams, and John Hancock.

Samuel Adams was the son of a wealthy businessman, but he had no knack for business. He had tried and failed at many things. It seemed that Sam Adams would never become successful at anything. Then the British Parliament passed the stamp and sugar taxes on the American colonies. Sam Adams soon discovered that he had a knack for organizing people in the colonies to oppose the unfair laws. He became a leader of a patriot organization called the Sons of Liberty and took a leading part in the Boston Tea Party. Sam Adams's fiery writings also helped stir up support for the patriot cause.

John Adams was Sam Adams's cousin. Thirteen years younger, he was a lawyer who had earned great respect among the colonists. He had been a leader in the protests against the Stamp Act and had supported the Boston Tea Party. He was opposed to violence, yet when the war broke out, he worked to get George Washington appointed commander of the Continental Army. He was known as "Old Sink or Swim" Adams because of his statement, "I will sink or swim, live or die, survive or perish with my country."

John Hancock was one of the wealthiest merchants in the American colonies. Hancock became a patriot leader after British customs officials caught the crew of his ship *Liberty* trying to bring a shipment of wine into Massachusetts without paying taxes on it. The officials charged Hancock with smuggling. John Adams agreed to be his lawyer. The charges were dropped, but Hancock soon was won over to the patriot cause by Sam Adams.

Another important patriot was Thomas Paine. Born in England, Paine had tried and failed at many professions before chance brought him to the attention of Benjamin Franklin, one of Pennsylvania's patriot leaders. In 1774 Franklin arranged for Paine to travel to Philadelphia and get work as a writer and editor. When war broke out, Thomas Paine found the work he was meant to do. In January of 1776, Paine's pamphlet *Common Sense* was published, with the help of Franklin and another Philadelphia patriot, Dr. Benjamin Rush. In the pamphlet, Paine put in words what many others were thinking— that the American colonies had no choice but to declare their independence from England.

In the summer of 1776, the spirit of independence grew throughout the colonies. Delegates from the colonies met in Philadelphia at the Second Continental Congress. They decided it was time to make a formal declaration about why they would no longer obey King George III and the British Parliament. John Hancock was the president of the Congress. Other members included John and Samuel Adams, Benjamin Franklin, Benjamin Rush, the wealthy Pennsylvania patriot Robert Morris, and Richard Henry Lee and Thomas Jefferson of Virginia. Thomas Jefferson was the author of a number of important writings on law, politics, and education. It was no surprise when he was chosen by Congress to write what came to be one of the greatest documents in history—the Declaration of Independence.

Here is a calendar of events of the Second Continental Congress during those fateful days.

June 7 Richard Henry Lee of Virginia proposes a resolution saying "that these United Colonies are and of rights ought to be, free and independent states."

June 10 A vote on the Lee resolution is delayed for three weeks so that the delegates can return to their colonies and discuss it with the colonial leaders. Meanwhile, Congress appoints a committee of five to write what will become the Declaration of Independence. Thomas Jefferson is the chairman.

June 28 Jefferson discusses the Declaration he has written with John Adams and Benjamin Franklin. The committee approves it.

July 1 Congress reconvenes.

July 2 The Lee resolution is passed by Congress.

July 3 Adams, Franklin, and Congress make a few small changes in the Declaration.

July 4 In the late afternoon Congress approves the Declaration. Church bells ring out.

July 5 Printed copies of the Declaration are sent out to all the colonies.

The Declaration of Independence stated, in carefully chosen and beautiful language, the patriots' ideas about the purpose of government and the reasons for the American colonies' declaration of independence.

With the Declaration of Independence, the delegates in Philadelphia created a new nation. Now there was no turning back. They would, indeed, have what Patrick Henry, years earlier, had called for—liberty or death.

Americans Make
a Revolution

WHEN THE AMERICAN REVOLUTION BEGAN in 1775 at Lexington, Massachusetts, most English citizens and many American colonists thought there was little chance the tiny, poorly trained patriot army could win the war.

England had many advantages. Its population was three times that of the American colonies. The British army was made up of professional soldiers who were led by experienced officers. The British navy, the largest in the world, commanded the seas. Great Britain could afford to supply and equip its army and navy and even hire foreign soldiers. Many Hessian soldiers—troops from the German state of Hesse—fought for the British in the American Revolution.

King George III knew that at least one-third of the colonists were still loyal to him. He thought of the revolution as a "little rebellion" that would be quickly put down. But he was wrong. The war lasted eight long, bloody years.

The American patriots had some advantages, too. They were fighting on their own ground, while the British had to fight 3000 miles away from their homeland. Also, many American fighters had rifles, firearms that were far more accurate than the muskets carried by the British soldiers. And American military leaders were better prepared to fight under unusual conditions than were the British generals. The Americans' greatest advantage was their commanding general, George Washington. He was a brilliant and brave soldier whose every act inspired his men in the long fight for liberty.

In March of 1776, Washington's troops forced the British out of Boston, but that summer the British decided to capture New York City and try to cut the colonial forces in two. General William Howe landed 10,000 men on Staten Island and prepared to attack Washington's army. Within weeks he increased his army to about 30,000. Unable to fight such a large British force, Washington sadly withdrew from New York City.

By the end of 1776, the Americans were discouraged. The war seemed mostly to have become one of defeat and retreat. Washington had crossed the Hudson River with his army into New Jersey and was retreating before the British army under General Charles Cornwallis.

But Washington was a master of surprises. That bitterly cold Christmas night, he and his army crossed the ice-choked Delaware River. The next morning they charged into Trenton, New Jersey. The amazed and bewildered Hessian troops quickly surrendered.

Washington scored another victory one week later at Princeton, New Jersey. In 1777 it began to look as if the Americans might win, after all. General Benedict Arnold became an American hero with a number of victories in northern New York. That summer the gallant and wealthy Marquis de Lafayette arrived from France with a shipload of men and supplies. He became a member of Washington's staff.

That September and October the Americans fought the British twice at Saratoga, New York. At the second Battle of Saratoga, the British General John Burgoyne was forced to surrender his army. This ended the British threat to divide the colonies. It was the greatest American victory so far and is considered by many the turning point of the American Revolution.

But General Arnold was unhappy and disappointed. Congress had passed him over for promotion several times, and he needed more money to pay for his expensive style of living. Later, in 1780, Arnold was given command of West Point, the American fortress on the Hudson River. That fall, American soldiers captured Major John André, the assistant to the British commander in New York City. André was returning from a secret meeting with Arnold. He was carrying a plan from Arnold that showed how the British could capture West Point. Arnold, once a hero, had turned traitor in return for money and a command in the British army. He escaped to England, but Major André was hanged as a spy.

The winter of 1777–1778 was extremely cold. Washington spent the bitter winter months with his troops at Valley Forge, Pennsylvania. The soldiers struggled to stay warm and find enough food to survive. Most of the men were poorly dressed for such hard conditions—many of them did not even have boots.

But the American army stayed together. A Prussian officer, General Friedrich Manfred von Steuben, drilled the patriot soldiers and turned them into a well-trained fighting force. Then, in February of 1778, the French government decided to support the American cause. Soon shiploads of supplies and French troops arrived.

In the fall of 1779 American spirits were boosted again when the American ship *Bonhomme Richard,* commanded by John Paul Jones, defeated the British ship *Serapis.* Now America was winning important battles at sea as well as on land.

The final American victory came in the fall of 1781, when Lord Cornwallis and his army were trapped at Yorktown, Virginia. A French fleet kept his army from escaping by sea, and American and French forces blocked the British on land. Cornwallis surrendered his army of 8000 to the Americans. The fighting was over.

In 1783 representatives from the United States and Great Britain met in Paris, France, and signed the treaty that ended the American Revolution. The United States gained new territory extending west to the Mississippi River. A new nation—and a new idea, government by the people—had come into the world.

A New Nation—
A New Constitution

THE DECLARATION OF INDEPENDENCE AND the struggle to win the American Revolution held the United States together, but only for a while. Most of the states opposed giving the federal government much power. But leaders such as Thomas Jefferson, Alexander Hamilton, and James Madison saw that the new federal government needed a strong set of laws by which the nation could be governed.

The first United States government had been established by the Articles of Confederation. They had been proposed by Richard Henry Lee of Virginia in 1777 and had gone into effect in 1781. From the beginning it was clear that the Articles did not give the national government the powers it needed to govern all the states equally and fairly. The individual states acted, as one critic said, like "13 independent Americas." They argued over boundaries, set up conflicting trade laws, and hardly acted like "united states" at all.

Alexander Hamilton was probably the greatest supporter of a strong central government. He proposed that delegates from all the states gather in Philadelphia in May, 1787, to work out a new Constitution—a set of laws that would give the national government the powers it needed yet would still be acceptable to the states. Reluctantly, the members of Congress called for such a meeting. George Washington left his Virginia home, Mount Vernon, for Philadelphia to preside over this Constitutional Convention.

The basic problem to be worked out was how to give the states equal power in the new Congress. If the number of representatives for each state were figured only according to the number of people in the states, then the states with the most people would have too much power in Congress. If each state were awarded the same number of representatives, then the states with the smallest number of people would have just as much power as the states with the most people, and that was not fair, either.

A compromise solved the problem. The delegates at the Philadelphia convention decided that the new Congress would have two parts—a House of Representatives and a Senate. In the House of Representatives, the number of representatives for each state would be figured according to the number of people in the state. In the Senate, each state would have two members, called *senators*.

The delegates at the Philadelphia convention also decided to divide the power of the federal government among three branches. Congress would be the *legislative branch* and have the power to pass laws, approve treaties, and raise money to pay government expenses. The President, the head of the *executive branch,* was given the power to negotiate treaties, command the army and navy, and sign or reject the laws passed by Congress. The Supreme Court, the highest court in the *judicial branch,* was given the power to decide whether laws are in agreement with the Constitution.

By dividing the powers and responsibilities among three different branches of government, the delegates to the Philadelphia convention created a system of *checks*

We the People of the United States, in order to form a more perfect Union, establish Justice, insure domestic Tranquility, provide for the common defence, promote the general Welfare, and secure the Blessings of Liberty to ourselves and our Posterity, do ordain and establish this Constitution for the United States of America.

and balances—power would be balanced among the branches, and each branch would act as a check against the others to keep them from becoming too powerful.

The Constitution included a way by which the citizens of the United States could *amend,* or change, the Constitution. This helped keep the real power of government under the control of the people, where it belongs in a true democracy.

The Constitution could become the law of the land only after nine of the thirteen states voted to *ratify,* or approve it. In December of 1787, Delaware became the first state to ratify the Constitution. A few days later, Pennsylvania became the second state to vote to ratify it. In June of 1788, New Hampshire became the ninth state to vote for ratification and the Constitution went into effect.

In April of 1789, George Washington, the hero of the American Revolution, was elected the first President of the United States under the new Constitution.

Many states, when they voted to ratify the Constitution, asked for changes, or amendments, that would state clearly the rights and freedoms of American citizens. Ten amendments, which came to be known as the Bill of Rights, were voted on by the state legislatures and became law in 1791.

The Constitution of the United States is a short, carefully planned set of laws. The delegates to the Constitutional Convention of 1787 had worked very hard to establish a form of government that would give the American people the freedom and democracy they had fought so hard to win. Over the years the people have voted to add new amendments, but even after more than 200 years, the Constitution is still the law of the land and one of the greatest documents ever written.

Eli Whitney—Inventor

BY THE LATE 1700's, Americans had already shown the world that they were an inventive people. After all, they had invented a brand new kind of government.

During colonial times, Americans had shown quite a knack for inventing. Even Benjamin Franklin had found time to invent many different things, including a new kind of heating stove and *bifocals,* eyeglasses that use one kind of lens for the lower halves and another kind for the upper halves.

In 1765, ten years before the American Revolution began, one of this nation's most important inventors was born on a farm near Westboro, Massachusetts. He was Eli Whitney, the son of Eli and Elizabeth Whitney.

From an early age, Eli was interested in mechanical things. When he was eight, he took apart his father's watch and put it back together in perfect running order. Another time, he examined a violin and then made his own violin. It proved to be a good instrument.

Young Eli spent much of his time in his father's workshop, fixing anything that needed repair. Realizing that Eli did his best work in the shop, his father let him tinker there while his younger brothers did all the farm chores. "You are a real handy man," Eli's father told him.

While working in his father's shop one day during the American Revolution, Eli thought of a way he could make money for the family. Because of the war, Americans could no longer get manufactured goods from England. Simple things such as nails were scarce and sold at high prices. Eli told his father that if he had a blacksmith's forge, he could make nails. His father supplied one and soon Eli was turning out nails and special tools that the farmers needed.

After the war was over, Americans went back to buying their manufactured goods from England, and Eli's business suffered. Although he had little money, Eli decided he must go to college. He worked hard and saved his money so he could afford a college education. Finally, in 1789, the same year that George Washington became the first President of the United States, Eli entered Yale College in New Haven, Connecticut.

When Eli graduated from college in 1792, he was offered a teaching job in Georgia. While traveling by boat to Savannah, Georgia, he met Mrs. Nathanael Greene, the widow of a great Revolutionary War general. Mrs. Greene was returning to her plantation in Georgia along with Phineas Miller, who ran the plantation. Soon the three were good friends.

When they got to Savannah, Eli Whitney learned that the teaching job that had been promised to him had been given to another teacher. He was without a job and was a long way from home. Mrs. Greene invited Eli to be a guest at her comfortable Georgia plantation. Eli gladly accepted her generous offer.

During his stay at the plantation, Eli tried to think of ways to thank Mrs. Greene for being so kind. He made her a pair of embroidery hoops. He mended the children's toys and made many other clever repairs. "Mr. Whitney," Mrs. Greene said, "you are a mechanical genius."

"Just a handy man," he replied.

One evening some neighboring plantation owners visited Mrs. Greene. "We must think of a crop we can grow or we will lose our plantations," they said.

"We could grow upland cotton," one of them said.

"Impossible," another replied. "It takes too long to pick the green, sticky seeds out of the cotton by hand, and no gin can be made that will seed it."

"Mr. Whitney could invent one," Mrs. Greene remarked.

"What is a gin?" Eli asked.

"Gin is short for engine," he was told.

Eli went to work on the problem. I could invent a machine with fine teeth that will pull the sticky green seeds from the cotton, he thought. He told Phineas Miller of his plan. Phineas raised money for the venture and the two men became business partners.

When the machine was finished, Mrs. Greene invited her planter friends to watch a demonstration. Eli's *cotton gin* worked. Many orders came in for the new gins, and soon everyone was planting vast fields of cotton—and buying slaves to work on their great plantations.

But there was trouble ahead. Even though Eli took out a government patent to protect his invention, the machine was easy for others to copy and build. Soon Eli was spending as much time in legal battles and in trying to get business loans as he was in building and improving his cotton gin.

The cotton gin was of great importance to the South, because it gave the Southern planters a crop they could sell at a great profit. But Eli Whitney and Phineas Miller made little profit from the cotton gin.

In 1798 Eli Whitney returned to Connecticut and looked for something new to invent. Once again Europe had become a battleground. The United States was faced with a possible war with France. Whitney knew the government needed muskets but could not buy them from Europe. Although he had never made a musket, he wrote to the government, stating that he could make and deliver up to 15,000 muskets if he had a contract and an advance of money. The United States government was desperate to have the muskets and accepted his offer.

Up to that time, each musket had been made by craftsmen who had fitted each part of the gun by hand. Whitney built machines that would make each part exactly the same every time. That meant that each part of each musket would fit on every other musket—all of the musket parts were *interchangeable.* The muskets could be produced in great numbers in factories.

Eli Whitney had invented the idea of *mass production.*

Within a few years, Whitney's factory was turning out great numbers of good muskets, and other businesses were beginning to use Whitney's system to manufacture many other kinds of things.

Eli Whitney's cotton gin had made the South a prosperous section of the country, but it had also given the idea of slavery new life. And his use of interchangeable parts in manufacturing revolutionized the industry of the North. Eli Whitney did not know it, but his inventions helped set the stage for the bloody clash between North and South—the Civil War.

The Louisiana Purchase

WHEN THOMAS JEFFERSON BECAME the third President of the United States, on March 4, 1801, the young nation stretched from the Atlantic Ocean to the Mississippi River, and from the Canadian border to the Spanish-owned colonies of East and West Florida. There were 16 states. The three new states that had been added to the original 13 were Vermont, Kentucky, and Tennessee. All three of these new states had been formed out of land belonging to the original colonies.

In 1801 the United States was faced with great opportunities but also with great dangers. Thomas Jefferson realized that his most important job as President was to keep the United States from getting involved in a war with any of the European nations. War meant hard times for farmers and businessmen, death, destruction, and possibly even invasion. Jefferson was determined to keep the country growing, prosperous, and at peace.

Spain's vast holdings in North America included the port city of New Orleans, located at the mouth of the great Mississippi River. This meant Spain was in a position to threaten the United States, for the nation that controlled New Orleans also controlled all the trade on the Mississippi River. In time of war, that nation could close the port and cripple the United States by stopping farmers from shipping and selling their produce and from receiving needed supplies. Happily for the United States, Spain was not strong enough to close New Orleans to American trade for long.

But Spain was not the only country that needed watching. Jefferson also kept a wary eye on the ambitious leader of France, Napoleon Bonaparte, who had said that he wanted to expand his country's colonies. New Orleans had once belonged to France. The city had many French citizens who hoped that New Orleans would once again come under French rule. Napoleon planned for this to happen, too.

On October 1, 1800, Napoleon signed a secret treaty with Spain. He agreed to help the king of Spain gain control of the territory of Parma, in northern Italy. In return, Spain would give France the territory of Louisiana, which stretched from New Orleans north to Canada, and as far west as the present states of Colorado, Wyoming, and Montana.

The king of Spain never did get his kingdom of Parma, but the Spanish were forced to turn Louisiana over to Napoleon anyway.

Once again France controlled New Orleans and had a vast colonial empire in North America. President Jefferson, and many other Americans, were shocked when they learned of the treaty between France and Spain.

Before the French took over, however, the Spanish officials in New Orleans closed the port to American shipping. But many American tradesmen and farmers thought the French had closed the port. They began to feel bitterly toward the French. Some people even talked of going to war and taking New Orleans by force.

Jefferson's worst fears appeared to be coming true. He sent James Monroe to France with instructions to try to buy the port of New Orleans. Monroe and the United States minister to France, Robert Livington, were given permission to offer Napoleon up to $10 million.

What Jefferson did not know was that Napoleon had decided to give up his dream of a French empire in North America. A bloody revolt on the French-owned island of Santo Domingo, in the Caribbean Sea, already had cost France a small fortune—and the lives of many of its best soldiers. And the almost continuous wars in Europe were an even greater burden.

Napoleon knew France could not afford to fight a war in Europe and also build an empire in North America. So he decided to sell the entire territory of Louisiana to the United States. In addition to raising needed money, the sale would keep France's enemy, England, from ever gaining control of Louisiana.

The day before James Monroe arrived in Paris, the French minister Talleyrand asked Robert Livingston how much the United States would pay for all of Louisiana.

Livingston learned that Napoleon wanted much more than he and Monroe were told to offer. But Monroe and Livingston knew that Louisiana was well worth the price. After two weeks of negotiations, they signed a treaty saying the United States would buy the entire territory for 80 million francs—about $15 million.

But even though the treaty had been signed, the sale still needed the approval of President Jefferson and the United States Congress. When Jefferson learned of the agreement, he was pleased. But some Americans were not so pleased. The businessmen of New England thought that the addition of the new Western lands would make their states less important and powerful. Many people thought that $15 million was too high a price to pay for a Western wilderness, no matter how big it was.

But in October of 1803, the United States Senate approved the purchase, and Louisiana became part of the United States.

Strangely enough, no one knew exactly how much land the United States had purchased or just what its boundaries were. But the Louisiana Purchase was one of history's greatest bargains. The United States had bought more than 565 million acres of new land and had more than doubled its size. The price worked out to about four cents an acre.

The United States now controlled the Mississippi River all the way to the sea, and the way was cleared for Americans to settle the West.

Texas
Gains Its Independence
and Joins the Union

WHEN THE UNITED STATES BOUGHT the territory of Louisiana in 1803, the treaty signed with France was not clear on the exact western boundary of the new territory. Some Americans thought it included part or all of the Spanish colony of Texas. In 1819 the United States signed a treaty settling the Louisiana boundary and stating that Texas belonged to Spain.

This treaty did not keep Americans from wanting to settle in Texas. Two years later, in 1821, a man named Stephen Austin led the first large group of American settlers—about 300 families—into Texas.

Stephen Austin's father, Moses Austin, had received permission to establish a colony of Americans in Texas but died before he could accomplish this. At the age of 27, Stephen Austin promised to carry on his father's work.

In the summer of 1821 Stephen Austin sent a small group of settlers by ship from New Orleans to Texas. They were to plant crops so that the whole colony would have food for the winter. But when Austin led a much larger group of settlers overland into Texas, they found no settlement, houses, or crops. The first group had landed in the wrong place.

Somehow Austin was able to keep the colony together and the settlers survived the first winter. Stephen Austin managed the affairs of the new colony wisely and soon it was strong and prosperous.

Stephen Austin's success led many more land-hungry Americans to Texas. But Texas was no longer a Spanish province. In 1821 the Spanish colony of Mexico had declared its independence of Spain. The new Mexican government passed laws making it easy for other American colonizers to receive large grants of land.

Within a few years, the number of Texas settlers who had come from the United States was greater than those who had come from Mexico. Even though most of the settlers were content under Mexican rule, some were not happy and tried to start a movement for independence. The Mexican government became alarmed. In 1830 it passed a law forbidding United States citizens from settling in Texas. The law ordered Mexican soldiers to Texas to make sure the laws of Mexico were obeyed.

This made the settlers already in Texas very unhappy. Sometimes fighting broke out between the Mexican soldiers and the settlers.

The Mexican officials feared that the American settlers would try to make Texas independent. The settlers thought the Mexican government would try to take their lands away and force them to leave Texas. Meanwhile, more people came to Texas from the United States. They settled wherever they wanted to, ignoring the wishes of the Mexican government.

In 1833 the soldier and politician Antonio López de Santa Anna became president of Mexico. Santa Anna increased his own power and authority until he was more of a dictator than a president. His harsh rule finally drove the Texas settlers into rebellion.

With a force of about 6000 troops, Santa Anna hurried north to put down the uprising. In February, 1836, Santa Anna trapped less than 200 Americans inside the Alamo,

an old mission in San Antonio, and began a siege that lasted 13 days.

The defenders in the Alamo, under the command of William Travis, included the famous frontiersmen Davy Crockett and James Bowie. Travis had been a lawyer and a political leader before the uprising against Santa Anna. Now he had the rank of colonel in the ragtag Texan army.

Travis knew that his little band was heavily outnumbered. Before Santa Anna's army surrounded the mission at San Antonio, he had sent riders to the other settlements asking for help and carrying the defiant message, "Victory or death!" But the other settlements, also facing attack, could send only a handful of volunteers.

The Texans were brave and clever fighters, but at last their ammunition ran out. Santa Anna gave the order to launch the final attack. "No prisoners," he instructed his troops. "They are all traitors and must be put to death."

All 187 of the Alamo defenders were killed. But it was a costly victory for the Mexican army. Nearly 1600 of Santa Anna's men lost their lives.

News of the massacre at the Alamo traveled through Texas. Angry settlers decided that the only course for Texas was independence. "Remember the Alamo" became the battle cry of Texas.

Santa Anna, who had called himself the Napoleon of the West, continued east to fight the rebellious Texans, confident that he would defeat all who opposed him.

In April, Santa Anna caught up with the main American army, led by Sam Houston, at the San Jacinto River in eastern Texas. Sam Houston had been an army officer, a congressman, and the governor of Tennessee. In the weeks following the Alamo disaster, Houston had been building up his army and waiting for the right moment to attack Santa Anna.

Houston led his small army in a surprise attack on the Mexican army. The Mexicans were caught off guard, and the battle was over in less than 30 minutes. Sam Houston had two horses shot out from under him and was badly wounded, but the Texans won.

Santa Anna escaped from the battle and tried to make his way to another Mexican army disguised in some old clothes. But he was captured and sent back to Sam Houston. Santa Anna was forced to sign a treaty granting Texas independence. He was eventually allowed to return to Mexico. The Mexican government refused to accept the treaty, but everyone knew the Texans had won their freedom.

Sam Houston was a hero in Texas. A few months later, a new town sprang up just a few miles north of the battleground. It was given the name Houston and was made the capital of the new Republic of Texas. And Sam Houston became the new nation's first president.

From 1836 to 1845 Texas remained an independent country. Even though the Mexican government still considered Texas as part of Mexico, it did not have enough money or troops to fight the Texans.

Many people in Texas thought that the young republic should become part of the United States. There were many people in the United States who agreed. On March 1, 1845, the United States Congress voted to *annex* Texas—to make it part of the United States. On December 29, 1845, Texas was admitted as the 28th state of the Union.

This made the Mexican government very angry. Soon a dispute over the boundary between the two countries led to fighting, and in 1846 the two nations went to war. Mexico was defeated, and in 1848 it signed a new treaty giving up its claim to Texas. Mexico also agreed to give the territories of New Mexico and California to the United States.

The United States had gained vast new lands and now stretched from the Atlantic Ocean to the Pacific Ocean.

ORIGINAL MORSE SENDER

Samuel Morse Invents
the Telegraph

IN THE EARLY COLONIAL DAYS it was difficult for people to get information about the events in other places. People got most of their news from letters or from talking with travelers.

The first newspaper to be printed in the colonies was published in Boston, Massachusetts, on September 25, 1690. The newspaper was called *Publick Occurrences.* It had only four pages, and one of the pages was left blank. The editor suggested that the reader write his or her own news items on the blank page before passing it along to the next reader.

This first newspaper lasted for only one issue, but as the years passed more and more newspapers were published. New highways and speedy railroads were built, linking the nation's towns and cities. Getting information quickly became much easier.

But in the early 1800's the United States grew by leaps and bounds, and it became more difficult for people in one part of the country to learn quickly what was happening in other parts of the country. A settler on the frontier who wanted to know about events in the East had to wait weeks or even months to find out. Newspapers or letters from the East had to be sent long distances over rough and unsettled land. And Easterners had to wait just as long for news about events in the West.

It was clear that the growing country needed a better and faster way to send information.

The person who finally invented the faster, better way was neither a scientist nor an inventer—he was a portrait painter named Samuel F.B. Morse.

In 1832 Morse was traveling across the Atlantic Ocean on the ship *Sully.* He was returning to the United States from Europe, where he had been living and studying.

One evening at dinner Morse had a conversation with some other passengers on the latest discoveries about electricity. Over the years, scientists had learned how to produce electricity from chemical batteries. They knew that electricity seemed to pass instantly through wires of any length. They also knew that by winding a coil of wire around a bar of soft iron and then running electricity through the wire, they could produce an *electromagnet.* This electromagnet could make the needle of a compass change its direction or attract an iron bar to it. And, they found, the electromagnet could be turned on and off simply by connecting or disconnecting the wire from the electric battery.

Suddenly the idea came to Samuel Morse that he could send messages over long distances of wire with electricity. He realized that he could send the letters and numbers in a sort of code, using long and short bursts of electricity. When the electricity got to the other end of the wire, an electromagnet would cause a pencil to make contact with a moving paper ribbon, and the message would be written down as dashes and dots. Anyone who knew the code could translate those dashes and dots back into the right letters and numbers—back into the original message!

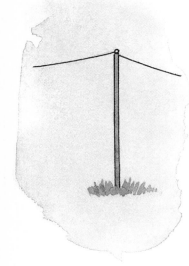

As soon as the ship docked in New York City, Samuel Morse set out to invent this new device, which he called the telegraph.

It took a long time for Morse to get the money he needed for his equipment and experiments. But he never gave up. He spent every spare minute and every spare penny on his telegraph.

In 1837 Morse demonstrated his new invention in New York, hoping that some businessmen would give him enough money to perfect the telegraph. Nobody was willing to invest in the telegraph, but a young student named Alfred Vail offered to help Morse build better versions of his telegraph equipment. Vail's family owned an iron works, and Morse gladly accepted. Soon Vail became Morse's partner.

The next year, Morse demonstrated his improved telegraph in Washington, D.C., but the government was no more interested in helping Morse than the businessmen in New York had been. Morse kept on working on his invention. He knew that some day he would be able to finish his telegraph.

At last, in 1843 Congress passed a bill granting money to build an experimental telegraph line from the Capitol Building in Washington, D.C., to Baltimore, Maryland. Morse was told this good news by Annie Ellsworth, the daughter of the commissioner of patents. Samuel Morse was so happy he promised Annie that she could choose the first message to be sent to Baltimore.

On May 24, 1844, the long telegraph wire from Washington to Baltimore was completed and Morse was ready to demonstrate his invention. Groups of people gathered at each of the telegraph stations, eager to see if Morse's telegraph would really work.

Morse took his place at the telegraph equipment in the Capitol Building, and Alfred Vail took up his post in Baltimore. It had been decided that Morse would send a message to Vail, and then Vail would send the same message back to Morse. Neither knew what message Annie Ellsworth had decided upon.

Annie gave Morse the message she had chosen, a verse from the Bible that read, "What hath God wrought."

Samuel Morse tapped out the message in dots and dashes, and the electric signals traveled along the wire to Baltimore. Then he sat back and waited for Alfred Vail's reply. About a minute later, Morse's receiving equipment began writing out the dots and dashes sent back by Vail. The excited group looked at the paper ribbon as Morse carefully translated the code back into letters: W-H-A-T . . . H-A-T-H . . . G-O-D . . . W-R-O-U-G-H-T.

The telegraph worked! Samuel Morse had "wrought" a wonderful invention.

Soon telegraph offices were being built in many towns and cities, all connected by hundreds of miles of wire.

It was not difficult to operate the telegraph or to learn the code that Morse had invented. Many telegraph operators soon learned that they could understand the code just by listening to the click-clack sounds of the receiving equipment. So the pencil and paper-ribbon receiver was replaced by the telegraph sounder.

New factories sprang up to provide the wire, batteries, keys, switches, sounders, telegraph poles—all the things needed by the growing telegraph industry.

One of the biggest jobs of all was putting up telegraph poles and stringing wires all the way across the United States. There were many problems. Buffalo liked to use the telegraph poles as back scratchers and often knocked poles down. The Indians came to hate the telegraph, for with it came new settlers, railroads, towns—and trouble.

After many hardships and setbacks, the telegraph was completed from coast to coast on October 24, 1861. Now Americans everywhere could send and receive messages across the country in an instant, thanks to the genius and hard work of Samuel Morse.

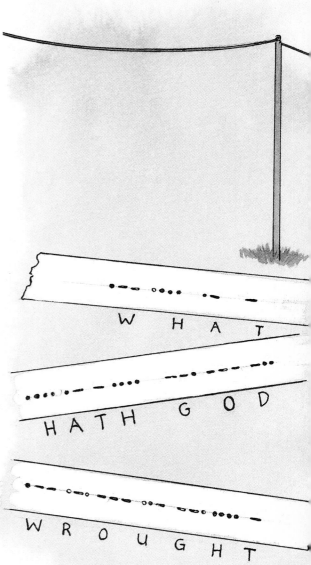

The Great California Gold Rush

CALIFORNIA TERRITORY IN THE 1840's was a vast frontier. Along its beautiful Pacific coastline there were missions and little villages that had been built by Spanish colonizers and missionaries. The families of some of the early Spanish settlers owned immense land grants, or ranchos. Life was unhurried, and the afternoon siesta, or nap, was a tradition.

Then one day something happened that was to change everything. On January 24, 1848, a man named James Marshall discovered rocks containing a yellow metal at the bottom of a river.

The metal was gold.

Marshall's employer was a hard-working California settler named John Sutter. Sutter had left Germany in search of a fortune. In 1839 he was granted a large tract of land by the Mexican governor of California. Sutter built a fort and began a settlement. Soon there were granaries, mills, and stores at the settlement, and Sutter became very wealthy.

Sutter hired James Marshall to build a sawmill on his property. The mill was built on the bank of the American River, not far from Sutter's Fort. The mill's great saw was to be powered by a waterwheel, and Marshall was busy deepening the channel, or mill race, for the waterwheel when he saw little flakes of gold in the hard, white, quartz rock that lined the riverbed.

Marshall told John Sutter about his discovery. Sutter had mixed feelings about the news Marshall brought him. He realized that the gold could make him fabulously wealthy, but it could also mean the destruction of the private, peaceful little empire he had built. He and Marshall agreed not to tell anyone about the discovery.

But the workers who helped Marshall build the sawmill could not keep the secret. Soon people from all over California were camping on Sutter's property, searching for gold.

The whole country learned of the discovery when President James K. Polk made his yearly message to Congress in December, 1848. Polk displayed a quantity of gold found in California and announced, "The accounts of the abundance of gold are of such extraordinary character as would scarcely command belief."

President Polk's message inspired thousands of people to set out for California to seek their fortunes, in what became known as the Gold Rush. In 1849 alone over 80,000 gold-hunters reached California.

Some of these adventurers—who came to be known as the Forty-Niners because the Gold Rush began in 1849—traveled by sea around South America's stormy Cape Horn. Others sailed to Panama, cut across the jungles of the Isthmus of Panama, and continued by ship once they reached the Pacific side of the isthmus. The largest number journeyed overland. Many died, but fortunately most—young, healthy, and determined—survived.

It seemed that the gold seekers would never stop coming, and there was good reason. The mother lode—the main source of the gold-bearing quartz—was discovered in 1850. It produced hundreds of millions of dollars worth of gold.

Most of the Forty-Niners were not lucky enough to find gold, but a few did "strike paydirt" and make their fortunes. Other Forty-Niners made money other ways—by working as bakers, doctors, carpenters, wagon drivers or

teamsters, dentists, hotelkeepers, newspaper publishers, storekeepers, farmers, and ranchers.

As the gold ran out and people got over their "gold fever," some of the disappointed prospectors packed up and traveled back to where they had come from. But many of the Forty-Niners stayed in California and helped build new towns, cities, ranches, farms, orchards, and vineyards.

What of John Sutter? His workers deserted him to search for gold themselves. He sold some of his land to gold seekers. Others simply seized what they wanted. Sutter was unable to stop the thousands of people who camped on his lands and dug, panned, or mined for gold. He went to the courts for help, but they would not honor his land claims—Sutter's original land grants were made by the Mexican government.

Finally, John Sutter moved to a small farm in Pennsylvania, but he never gave up his hope that the United States government would restore his lands to him. In 1880, on one of his many trips to Washington, D.C., John Sutter died.

James Marshall fared no better. He died in poverty in 1885. His grave is near the spot where he made his historic discovery.

Years before, Sutter and Marshall had met with the Indian tribe that controlled much of the gold-producing Sacramento Valley. An old chief of the tribe spoke words of warning: "The yellow metal my white friends seek is bad medicine. It belongs to an evil spirit who in the end devours all who search for it."

For Sutter and Marshall and many others these words came true, but for others the great Gold Rush brought good fortune. There were two sides to the bright gold coin James Marshall's discovery produced—happiness for some, heartbreak for others.

Today, California's capital city of Sacramento stands not far from the site of Sutter's Fort. And everywhere throughout California you can meet the descendants of the brave and adventurous Forty-Niners.

A House Divided

SEVERAL TIMES DURING THE 1800's, as the nation grew and new states were admitted to the Union, it seemed as though the issue of slavery would cause the United States to be split in two. Many people thought that slavery is wrong—that no person should be able to own another. Many others thought that slavery is not wrong, and that the government in Washington, D.C., should not try to tell the states what to do. After all, they argued, nowhere in the Constitution did the Founding Fathers say that slavery is wrong and should be ended, or abolished.

The states in the South relied on slaves to grow and gather their valuable cotton crops. They were eager to continue slavery. But in the industrial North, where there were no slaves, a movement was growing to abolish slavery everywhere in the United States.

In 1858 an Illinois lawyer who had served in Congress was nominated by the Republican Party for a seat in the United States Senate. His name was Abraham Lincoln. He had helped organize the Republican Party two years earlier. In the summer of 1858, Lincoln campaigned against a great Illinois politician named Stephen A. Douglas. Even though Douglas won the election, Lincoln impressed many people across the country with his sharp intelligence and wonderful speechmaking.

Above all, people remembered that Lincoln thought slavery to be a great wrong. He also said that the United States could not remain half-free and half-slave. Quoting from the Bible, Lincoln said, "A House divided against itself cannot stand." Eventually the Union would have to permit slavery everywhere or it would have to forbid it everywhere.

In 1860 the Republican Party nominated Lincoln as their candidate for the Presidency. The Democratic Party nominated Lincoln's old opponent, Stephen Douglas.

Even though Lincoln did not think the federal government should interfere with slavery where it already existed, he thought it should not be permitted in new states or territories. This angered many Southerners, who believed that Lincoln really wanted to abolish slavery everywhere. Many Southern politicians swore that if Lincoln were elected President, their states would vote to *secede,* or leave the Union.

On November 6, 1860, Lincoln was elected, soundly defeating Stephen A. Douglas and two other candidates.

When Lincoln took the oath of office as President of the United States on March 4, 1861, seven Southern states—South Carolina, Mississippi, Florida, Alabama, Georgia, Louisiana, and Texas—had already decided to secede from the Union. Delegates from the seceding states had met in Montgomery, Alabama, and had voted to form a new nation, the Confederate States of America.

The delegates elected Jefferson Davis, a congressman from Mississippi, to be president of the Confederacy. Davis had often defended the rights of states to run their own affairs—especially in the matter of slavery.

Soon Confederate soldiers and officials began taking over federal forts and arsenals and forcing the Union troops to leave. Lincoln tried not to do anything that would anger the Southerners, but he was determined to

hold on to the Union forts and supply the troops defending them. He did not want to start a bloody civil war, but he had sworn to keep the Union together.

Early in the morning of April 12, 1861, Confederate forces in Charleston, South Carolina, opened fire on Fort Sumter, the Union fort in Charleston harbor. The Confederates had learned that a Union ship was on its way to the fort. They thought the ship was bringing more troops and stocks of ammunition and they wanted to capture the fort before the ship could arrive. In fact, the ship was only carrying food and supplies.

The next day, after 34 hours of battle, the commander of the fort surrendered.

The Civil War had begun.

President Lincoln called for 75,000 volunteer troops to put down the rebellion of the Southern states. He also ordered the United States Navy to blockade the Confederate ports. These actions caused four more states—Virginia, Arkansas, Tennessee, and North Carolina—to join the Confederacy.

When the citizens of Charleston had seen the American flag taken down at Fort Sumter and the white flag of surrender go up, they had joined the Confederate troops

and cheered happily. They did not know that this tiny Confederate victory would bring four years of bloody, brutal war—and that more than 600,000 Americans would die.

At the beginning of the war, the Confederacy won many important battles. The Union army had more troops, guns, and supplies, but the Confederate army had better generals. As the war continued, one Confederate general, Robert E. Lee, rose to become the greatest general in the Confederate army. Many times, Lee's brilliant strategies helped the Confederate army to beat larger and better prepared Union forces.

Lee's best general was a cavalry officer named Thomas Jonathan Jackson. He was called Stonewall Jackson because once, in a battle, he had stood his ground on the battlefield like a stone wall, paying scarce notice to the bullets whizzing all around him.

Jackson could move his troops great distances in very little time, and his troops fought like tigers. Lee could always rely on Stonewall Jackson, and the two generals gave the South some great victories. But in May of 1863,

at the great and terrible Battle of Chancellorsville, Stonewall Jackson was accidentally shot by his own troops. He died eight days later. When Lee heard of Jackson's death, he said, "I feel as though I have lost my right arm."

Lee had other good generals but he was never able to find anyone who could take Jackson's place. And time was working against the Confederacy. Every day the Union army received more troops and weapons, and every day the Confederate army became smaller and weaker. The Union's naval blockade was slowly starving the Confederacy.

On January 1, 1863, President Lincoln had issued the Emancipation Declaration, which said that all the slaves in territories held by the Confederacy were freed. But Lincoln knew that if the proclamation were to mean anything, the Confederacy had to be defeated.

Fortunately for the Union, Lincoln had found his own great general—Ulysses S. Grant. Grant knew that the Union had more of everything than the South, so he planned to beat Lee by wearing the Confederate army down. Grant forced the Confederates to fight and tried to keep them tied down and unable to move. His strategy worked. In the spring of 1865, Grant trapped Lee's army in Virginia, near the little town of Appomattox. On April 9, 1865, Lee surrendered his army to Grant.

The Civil War was over. Soon slavery was outlawed and the job of rebuilding the nation was begun.

But Abraham Lincoln was not among the rebuilders. On April 14, 1865, he had been shot while watching a play at Ford's Theater in Washington, D.C. Americans everywhere mourned the death of the President who had saved the Union.

The Transcontinental Railroad Links East and West

LONG BEFORE THE GOLD RUSH OF 1848, Americans had wished for a shorter and faster way to get to the West Coast of the United States.

There were three routes from the East, and all were quite slow. The first way to travel was by ship along the Atlantic coast of South America, around Cape Horn, and then back north by way of the Pacific Ocean. This trip took several months. The coming of sleek, fast vessels called clipper ships reduced the sailing time to California, but the trip was still very long.

Another route to California was by ship to Central America and the Isthmus of Panama. Travelers would leave the ship and travel by land across the isthmus. When they reached the Pacific Ocean, they would board another ship for the final voyage to California. This route was shorter and faster, but it was still long and tiring.

Travelers could also make the trip to California overland, by horse or oxen-drawn wagons across the plains, mountains, and desert. In many ways this was the most difficult and dangerous way of all.

But some people dreamed of a quicker, easier way to travel west—by rail! By 1850 all the big cities east of the Mississippi River had been connected to each other by a great network of railroads. The Iron Horse, as the railroad locomotive was called, had made it easy to travel from one place to another. Why not build a railroad all the way across the great West and into California?

In the 1850's the United States Army surveyed possible routes for such a transcontinental railroad. But the West was sparsely populated. No one could see how a railroad could pay for itself with so few passengers.

Then, in May of 1861, only a month after the Civil War began, Congress passed the Homestead Act. This law provided 160 acres of public land in the West to anyone who settled on that land for five years and improved it.

Because of the Homestead Act, land-hungry settlers began to flock to the Western lands and new farms and settlements sprang up. Farmers and ranchers needed to get their products to market, and settlers needed to buy products manufactured in the East. Soon there would be a real need for a railroad.

Abraham Lincoln saw a transcontinental railroad as a way to tie the Western territories more closely to the Union. But he knew the government could not fight the Civil War and built the railroad at the same time.

Lincoln was not the only person who dreamed of a transcontinental railroad. In California, a man named Theodore Judah had worked for years to get Congress to build a railway from California to the East. In 1859 he finally succeeded in talking four businessmen into building a railroad from Sacramento to the gold and silver mines in the Sierra Nevada mountains. The four men were Leland Stanford, Charles Crocker, Mark Hopkins, and Collis P. Huntington, and their new company was called the Central Pacific Railroad.

Judah returned to Washington, D.C., and finally got Congress interested in building a transcontinental railroad. In 1862 Congress passed a bill that created a new railroad company, the Union Pacific Company.

The Union Pacific was awarded a contract to build a railroad westward from Omaha, Nebraska. The Central Pacific Company was given a contract to build a railroad eastward from Sacramento, California. The two companies would work toward each other and would eventually join their rail lines. To help pay the enormous cost of building the railroad, the government agreed to give the railroad companies large tracts of land along the railroad path, or right of way. It also agreed to lend them money they would need to build the railroad.

On January 9, 1863, the first shovelful of earth was turned in Sacramento, and the great building race between the Union Pacific and Central Pacific began.

There were many problems. Millions of steel rails and wooden railroad ties and thousands of tons of food and supplies had to be shipped great distances. Tunnels and winding railroad beds had to be carved out of solid rock in the high Sierra Nevada mountains. Bridges had to be built across steep and deadly mountain passes.

All this work meant the railroads had to hire many thousands of workers and then feed, clothe, and house them as they pushed the tracks forward. The Civil War drew many able-bodied workers into the Union and Confederate armies, and work on the Union Pacific was delayed for years. On the Central Pacific, the workers who were hired usually deserted their railroad jobs as soon as they got into the gold and silver fields in California and Nevada.

At last, the chief engineer of the Central Pacific hired a group of Chinese workers. They toiled from dawn to dusk for very little pay, and they did not quit. Soon there were thousands of Chinese workers helping to build the Central Pacific Railroad.

The Union Pacific hired thousands of tough, hard-working Irish laborers. After the Civil War ended, they were joined by battle-hardened ex-soldiers—many of them former Confederates.

Day by day, and mile by mile, the two great railroad gangs worked their way across the American frontier. Year after year they hammered and hauled and drilled and dug. Slowly the two rail lines stretched closer and closer to each other. Then, in the early spring of 1869, the rail crews came within sight of each other.

The great day finally arrived for the joining of the railroad from the West to the railroad from the East. The two tracks had come together at a level valley in the Utah desert north of Great Salt Lake, at a place called Promontory Point.

On May 10, 1869, a great crowd of workers, politicians, railroadmen, and reporters gathered at Promontory Point to see the driving of the last spike and the joining of the two railroads. Leland Stanford, head of the Central Pacific, was given the honor of driving the spike, which was made of gold. On either side, a mighty locomotive breathed smoke and hissed steam. And all around, the people who had gathered waited quietly.

Stanford lifted a silver-plated hammer, swung it over his shoulder—and missed the spike! Thomas Durant,

head of the Union Pacific, took the hammer and swung, and he missed, too. Finally, Grenville Dodge, the chief engineer of the Union Pacific, drove the spike into place.

Over the telegraph line this message was tapped out: "The last rail is laid . . . the last spike driven . . . the Pacific Railroad is completed." The Atlantic Coast and the Pacific Coast were linked with bands of steel.

The New Wave of Immigration

Give me your tired, your poor,
Your huddled masses, yearning to breathe free,
The wretched refuse of your teeming shore.
Send these, the homeless, tempest-tossed to me,
I lift my lamp beside the golden door!

THESE STIRRING WORDS are from a poem by Emma
Lazarus. They were inscribed on the base of the Statue
of Liberty in 1903. "Lady Liberty," as the statue is sometimes called, stands on an island in New York Harbor,
facing out toward the open sea. Given to the United
States by France on July 4, 1883, the Statue of Liberty has
welcomed millions of people who traveled from many
nations to start new lives in the United States.

The United States has received a larger number of
immigrants than any other country in the history of the
world. This nation has been called a nation of immigrants
because most Americans can trace their family history
back and find ancestors who came from Europe, Asia, or

Africa. Even the ancestors of the American Indians traveled to America from Asia, across a land bridge that once connected Siberia and Alaska.

In the 1600's most of the explorers who visited and colonists who settled the new land were English, French, Spanish, and Dutch. Today we can easily see their influence in building America. For example, New York was named after York in England. New Orleans was named after the French city of Orleans, and Louisiana was named for King Louis XIV of France. Florida is actually a Spanish word meaning "flowering." And who can read Washington Irving's tales about Rip Van Winkle and the Headless Horseman and not think of the Dutch settlement of New Netherland?

Other groups also came to America during this time. William Penn, the founder of Pennsylvania, wrote many inspiring pamphlets about the beauty and richness of his colony, and these were printed in many languages throughout Europe. Many Germans read Penn's pamphlets and decided to make the long journey to Pennsylvania. These settlers were called the *Pennsylvania Deutsch,* because "Deutsch" is the German word for "German." But in time other people forgot this, and the settlers came to be known as the *Pennsylvania Dutch,* even though they were not Dutch at all.

In the 1700's new settlers—most from England and other European countries—came to the American colonies. This steady stream of immigrants stopped for a time during the American Revolution. But in the 1820's more and more people started to arrive in the new land of freedom—most of them from the crowded countries of Europe.

In the 1830's almost 600,000 immigrants came to America. In the 1840's the growing stream of immigrants became a flood—more than 1.7 million people came to the United States, mostly from Ireland, where millions were dying from starvation, and Germany, where a great revolution had risen and then had been crushed by the armies of the European kings.

Every year, more and more immigrants arrived in the United States, some seeking jobs, some seeking land to farm, but all seeking freedom and hope. In 1873 alone, almost 500,000 newcomers arrived. By 1882 the number was nearly 800,000.

More than 14 million European immigrants came to the United States between 1860 and 1900. Many of these arrivals had relatives or friends already living in the country. There were many, however, who knew no one. They were poor, but they had saved up enough money to pay for their passage aboard a crowded steamship. By the time they reached the United States, they were almost penniless, but they had faith that they would soon find work in this new land of opportunity.

Some went to work in factories in the large cities. Others pushed on west and started up their own farms.

The pioneer farmers of the Great Plains often built their first houses out of sod—prairie grass cut out of the ground in blocks. These farm families endured severe winters, loneliness, and the difficulty of learning a new language and new customs. It was not an easy life but for many it was a rewarding one.

By the 1890's most newcomers to the United States were still coming from Europe, but they were coming from different countries—the countries of southern and eastern Europe. Now the Statue of Liberty greeted millions of weary travelers from Italy, Greece, the great Austro-Hungarian Empire, Poland, and Russia.

These new immigrants were not welcomed by all Americans, however. The United States had grown large and strong. American workers were fighting for higher wages and better working conditions. Many were afraid that the new immigrants would accept poor working conditions and lower wages. To many who had already settled in the United States, the newcomers were a threat. They were often greeted with hostility and resentment.

As time went by, the United States government passed new laws that limited immigration. The number of people coming to the United States dropped to a small fraction of what it had been. But after World War II immigration rose sharply, as thousands of European refugees and displaced persons sought the United States as a haven. In the 1960's, new rules made it easier for people from other countries to come and live in the United States. Now more than 500,000 newcomers—many from Mexico, Asia, India, and nations in the Caribbean Sea—arrive in the United States every year.

Immigrants have made many important contributions to life in the United States. Science, the arts, government, and industry have been enriched by the brave people who left the familiar lands of their birth for this land of promise. An "Immigrant Hall of Fame" would include such famous people as John J. Audubon, Albert Einstein, Alexander Graham Bell, Andrew Carnegie, Irving Berlin, Knute Rockne, and Elizabeth Taylor, to name only a very few.

The United States Becomes a World Power

IN THE YEARS FOLLOWING the Civil War, the United States grew into a great nation. The railroads stretched into the West, opening up new lands for farmers and ranchers. Immigrants by the thousands took up jobs in the steel mills, textile mills, and factories. The United States became rich by selling manufactured goods, steel, wheat, cotton, and a thousand other things to nations around the world.

Toward the end of the 1890's, the United States was ready to become a world power. Its great wealth and industry made it strong in the world of business.

Inventions such as John Ericsson's ironclad warship *Monitor* had also helped the United States to become a strong military power. Ericsson had invented the *Monitor* during the Civil War. In the years that followed, the United States had steadily built up a fleet of powerful, modern warships. The United States Navy helped protect American interests around the world.

For many years the United States government had watched with growing alarm the actions of Spain toward its last large colony in the New World, Cuba. For many

years, Cuban patriots had tried to win their island's independence from Spain. The Spanish government refused to give up its profitable colony. The Cuban revolutionaries were not strong enough to defeat the Spanish soldiers, but Spain was not strong enough to defeat the Cuban revolutionaries, either.

Year after year the fighting continued. The United States government tried to get Spain to grant Cuban independence but had no success. Relations between the two countries got worse. Then several U.S. newspapers began publishing sensational articles about Spanish cruelty toward Cuban and American citizens. Most of these stories were untrue, but they enraged Americans.

President William McKinley wanted to avoid an expensive and bloody war with Spain, and so did most members of Congress. But it was clear that something had to be done. On January 25, 1898, the United States battleship *Maine* steamed into the harbor of Havana, Cuba. Its mission was to protect the Americans in Cuba.

On the night of February 15, 1898, less than a month after the *Maine* had arrived in Havana harbor, a mysterious explosion ripped through the hull of the great warship. The ship sank, killing 260 officers and crewmen.

Most Americans believed that Spain was responsible for the explosion. The Navy investigated the sinking of the *Maine.* It decided that the *Maine* had been sunk by an underwater bomb, but could not show that Spain was responsible. But newspaper headlines across the country declared that Spanish agents had sunk the battleship. "Remember the *Maine*" became a battle cry, and many Americans demanded war with Spain.

On April 25 the United States declared war on Spain.

The war lasted only 113 days, and the first important battle was fought not in Cuba but in Spain's colony in the Pacific, the Philippines. On May 1, an American fleet commanded by Commodore George Dewey sailed into the harbor at Manila, the capital of the Philippines, and prepared to fight the Spanish fleet anchored there. When the U.S. squadron came close enough to the Spanish ships, Dewey gave the order to the captain of his flagship, "You may fire when you are ready, Gridley." In seven hours the Spanish fleet was destroyed, and Dewey had not lost a single man in the battle.

This victory was brought about in part because of the efforts of the assistant secretary of the Navy, Theodore Roosevelt. He had seen trouble coming and had ordered the Pacific squadron to be ready to fight. But by the time Commodore Dewey had sailed into Manila Bay, Teddy Roosevelt had already resigned from the government. He and his friend, Dr. Leonard Wood, were busy raising a regiment of volunteers to fight in Cuba.

Many of Roosevelt's admirers rushed to sign up as members of the cavalry regiment, which came to be known as the "Rough Riders." They were backwoodsmen from Maine, cowboys from the West, college boys from Harvard, and many others. They trained in Texas, moved on to Florida, and then shipped out to Cuba.

In July, 1898, Theodore Roosevelt and the Rough Riders played an important part in the Battle of San Juan Hill and the capture of the important city of Santiago. By the time Roosevelt got back to New York City, he was a national hero.

In December, Spain signed a peace treaty with the United States, and the Spanish-American War was over. Cuba was granted its independence. The United States gained the Philippines and the Pacific island of Guam, as well as the Caribbean island of Puerto Rico.

During the war, the United States Navy had used the Hawaiian islands as a base for refueling and resupplying its ships. Hawaii's importance to the Navy helped convince Congress to vote to annex Hawaii and make it part of the United States. In July of 1898, two months after Commodore Dewey's victory at Manila, Congress annexed Hawaii. It became a territory in 1900.

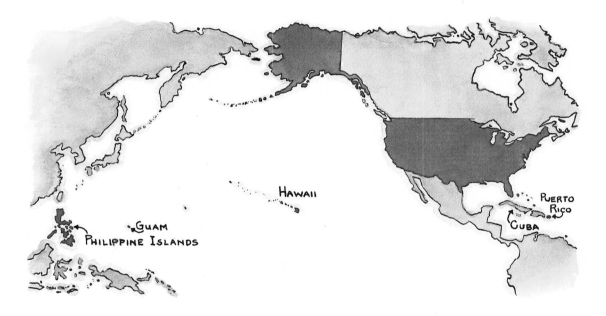

Suddenly the United States was a world power. The Spanish-American War brought the nation new influence in world affairs. Americans felt very good about their country and their President. In 1900 William McKinley was reelected to the Presidency, and his Vice President was none other than Teddy Roosevelt.

Then, on September 6, 1901, President McKinley was shot by an assassin. When McKinley died eight days later, Theodore Roosevelt became the nation's 25th President. He was 42 years old, the youngest President ever to enter the White House.

The Wright Brothers and the Age of Flight

PEOPLE HAVE ALWAYS DREAMED of flying. The wonder of flight has been recounted in stories of winged horses, winged dragons, and even magic flying carpets.

One of the first serious thinkers about air flight was the Italian artist and inventor Leonardo da Vinci, who lived from 1452 to 1519. He invented a parachute and also fashioned a model for a helicopter. But in Leonardo's day there were no engines to power his helicopter, so he was never able to test it.

Other pioneers in flight included two Frenchmen, the brothers Joseph and Etienne Montgolfier. In 1783 the Montgolfiers flew a balloon filled with hot air over the city of Paris. Their balloon flight was the first aerial voyage by humans.

In America, the first manned balloon flight was made on January 9, 1793, by a Frenchman, François Blanchard, at Philadelphia, which was then the capital of the United States. President Washington was there for the occasion.

In the 1800's many people experimented with hot-air balloons, gas-filled balloons, and gliders. Scientists and experimenters studied the wings and tails of birds in order to learn how the birds were able to fly. By the end of the 1800's, a number of people were building and testing gliders that were able to rise off the ground in a strong wind.

In Dayton, Ohio, two brothers named Wilbur and Orville Wright were experimenting with gliders of their own. The Wright brothers owned a bicycle shop in Dayton. They spent every spare minute building and experimenting with gliders, and learning everything they could about flight.

In 1900 the Wright brothers traveled to Kitty Hawk, a town on the coast of North Carolina, to continue their glider experiments. The large sandy hills overlooking the beach near Kitty Hawk were excellent launching places for gliders. Kitty Hawk's steady, strong sea breeze was excellent for lifting their gliders into the air. The Wright brothers learned so much at Kitty Hawk that they returned in 1901, and again in 1902, to continue their experiments.

Slowly but surely, Orville and Wilbur Wright were adding to the world's knowledge of flight. They made more than 1000 short flights in their gliders and kept careful records of all they learned. They invented many new features to help control gliders in flight.

The Wright brothers knew that they could not always rely on the wind to lift their glider into the air. What they needed was an engine powerful enough to *propel* the machine through the air, just as a ship's engine propels the ship through the water. The problem was that all the engines available were too heavy. They would act more like anchors than engines.

Orville and Wilbur finally decided they would have to design and build their own engine.

Finally, after much work and many trials and failures, the Wright brothers believed they had the right glider and the right engine to lift them into the air.

They returned to Kitty Hawk in the fall of 1903 and got ready to test their improved air machine.

On the morning of December 17, the brothers and their air machine were ready. Orville climbed onto the craft, lying face down on its lower wing.

The 12-horsepower engine sputtered to life and the air machine moved forward. Then, in one magical moment, it lifted itself off the ground. Orville flew a distance of 120 feet, staying aloft for 12 seconds.

A person had flown in a heavier-than-air machine!

Then, after the brothers made a few repairs to the aircraft, Wilbur took his turn. He climbed into the pilot's position, and again the machine pulled itself forward and lifted into the salty air of Kitty Hawk. Wilbur flew about 175 feet. Then it was Orville's turn again and he flew more than 200 feet.

Finally, Wilbur made the fourth and final flight, and it was the best of all. Wilbur flew 852 feet and stayed aloft for 59 seconds—almost a full minute!

The Wright brothers had turned a page in the history of the world. The age of powered flight had begun.

Orville and Wilbur continued to improve their air machine. In 1905 alone they made or attempted 105 flights. Then, in 1907, President Theodore Roosevelt read an article about the Wright brothers in the magazine *Scientific American.* Soon the government invited the Wrights to build an airplane for the Army Signal Corps.

The airplane had to carry two people, maintain an average speed of 40 miles an hour, and carry enough fuel for a flight of 125 miles.

The first demonstration flight of the military plane took place at Fort Myer, Virginia, on September 3, 1908. On September 9, Orville flew over the test field for more than an hour, at an altitude of 120 feet. The Wright flying machine was a success. Orville and Wilbur Wright now had a government contract that assured them financial success.

The original Wright Flyer, which the brothers had flown at Kitty Hawk in December, 1903, is in the National Air Museum in Washington, D.C. Thousands of people come each year to see the marvelous machine built by two brothers from Dayton, Ohio.

In 1935 a memorial was placed on a tall sandy hill near Kitty Hawk honoring the two brave men who, on a cold December day in 1903, began the Age of Flight.

America and the War to End Wars

IN THE EARLY 1900's, while the Wright brothers were improving their airplane, the United States was growing into an important world power. Factories were humming day and night, producing thousands of different things for sale around the world. The strong United States Navy helped protect the ships that carried those goods abroad and also the American citizens and businesses in other countries.

In 1905 President Theodore Roosevelt played an important role in ending a war between Russia and Japan. A few years later he sent an American fleet on a cruise around the world. The battleships and cruisers were painted white, and the fleet came to be called the Great White Fleet.

One of President Roosevelt's favorite sayings was, "Speak softly and carry a big stick." This was his way of saying that the United States wanted peace, but it would not be bullied by other countries.

In Europe, however, the threat of war had been growing for many years. The European countries had formed many alliances, or agreements to come to the aid of one another if war should break out. This meant that if two small nations went to war, even the great European empires might become involved.

That is exactly what happened in the summer of 1914. The heir to the throne of the Austro-Hungarian Empire, Archduke Francis Ferdinand, was assassinated. The young revolutionary who killed the archduke, Gavrilo Princip, had wanted to help the small nation of Serbia—which is now part of Yugoslavia—in its struggles against Austria-Hungary.

Almost immediately Austria-Hungary declared war on Serbia. Russia soon came to the aid of Serbia. Germany quickly declared war on Russia and then on France. Then Great Britain declared war on Germany. Other nations became involved in the war—Italy, Bulgaria, Belgium, Japan, the Ottoman Empire. The little war between Austria-Hungary and Serbia grew into a world war.

The nations of Europe divided into two warring groups. Germany joined Austria-Hungary, the Ottoman Empire, and other nations to form the Central Powers. Great Britain joined France, Russia, and other nations to form the Allied Powers, or Allies.

In the United States most people wanted the nation to stay out of the conflict in Europe. Many people favored the cause of the Allies, and many others leaned to the German and Austrian side. But very few people wanted American soldiers to fight in a war in Europe.

Woodrow Wilson was the President of the United States when the war broke out. He felt strongly that the United States should remain neutral and avoid entering the war on either side. But a series of events forced him to change his mind.

In February of 1915, Germany announced that it would use its fleet of submarines to blockade Great Britain. The next month, a German submarine sank the British passenger ship *Falaba.* Among the passengers who were killed was a United States citizen. In May, the American ship *Gulflight* was torpedoed. It did not sink, but three Americans were killed.

Then one of Great Britain's largest and most luxurious passenger ships, the *Lusitania,* sailing from the United States to England, was torpedoed and sunk off the Irish coast. Over 1000 of its passengers and crew died. Among the dead were 128 American citizens.

Americans were outraged by the sinking of the *Lusitania.* Many people wanted the United States to declare war on Germany and the Central Powers. President Wilson told Germany that the United States would not accept such attacks upon its citizens.

The Germans finally agreed not to sink any more passenger ships, but the submarine war continued. More ships were torpedoed, and more American lives were lost.

In 1917 Germany told the United States that it would once again sink any ships traveling to or from Great Britain. Then the United States learned that Germany had offered to help Mexico reconquer parts of the United States if the United States should join the Allies.

In 1916 Woodrow Wilson had been reelected as "the President who kept us out of war." But he could do so no longer. On April 2, 1917, he asked Congress to declare war on Germany.

General John J. Pershing was appointed to command the American Expeditionary Force, which was to be sent to fight in Europe. The first American soldiers, or *dough-boys,* arrived in France in June of 1917. Many remembered that the French had helped the United States in the American Revolution. One of Pershing's officers, visiting the grave of the Marquis de Lafayette in Paris, announced, "Lafayette, we are here!" Now it was time for the Americans to help the French.

Almost 1.5 million American soldiers served in France, where millions of soldiers had fought and died since the guns started firing in 1914. Both sides were worn out by the war, but neither side had been able to defeat the other. Then the fresh, determined American troops began to turn the tide in favor of the Allies.

In November of 1918, the Germans asked for an *armistice,* an end to the fighting. At 11 o'clock on the morning of November 11—the eleventh hour of the eleventh day of the eleventh month—the fighting stopped.

President Wilson had hoped to make this world war the "war to end war." He had hoped the nations of Europe would sign a peace treaty that was so just and fair that they would never again want to go to war. But the peace treaty that was signed at Versailles, France, in 1919 was not fair. It placed the blame for the war on Germany and forced it to accept a harsh punishment.

But the treaty did establish a new organization, the League of Nations, which President Wilson had proposed. In the League of Nations, leaders from all nations, big and small, could meet together and try to settle their disagreements peacefully.

President Wilson worked very hard to make the United States a member of the League of Nations, and he was heartbroken when the United States Senate voted against joining.

The League of Nations was not able to end war, but Wilson's dream of world peace did not die. In 1945 a new organization, the United Nations, took up Woodrow Wilson's dream, and the United States was one of its first members.

Lucky Lindy and
the Jazz Age

THE WORLD WAR CAUSED MANY CHANGES in the way people lived and thought. One of the biggest changes was in the way they thought about war. There had been too many deaths and too much destruction. Most people did not want to think about war at all. They wanted to get on with their lives—and have a little fun, too.

One of the new forms of fun was the air show. During the war many improvements had been made to the airplane, and many young men had learned how to fly as Army pilots. When they returned home, some took jobs with the Post Office, flying mail by air from city to city. Others bought old Army planes and traveled across the country, flying in air shows and races.

During the exciting years of the 1920's, these young pilots learned important things about how to make airplanes stronger and safer. Soon airplanes were flying higher, faster, and farther than ever before.

The great dream of pilots in those days was to fly a plane from the United States to Europe across the Atlantic Ocean—a distance of more than 3000 miles. Such a long flight seemed impossible to most people, but a few airplane builders and pilots knew that some day it would be done.

In 1919 Raymond Orteig, an aviation enthusiast, had offered a prize of $25,000 to the first person to fly non-stop from New York City to Paris, France. Years passed, but no one succeeded in making the flight. Finally, a young airmail pilot from the Midwest, Charles A. Lindbergh, made up his mind to win the prize.

First he studied what type of plane and motor would be best for the long transatlantic flight. After careful study, he decided that a new type of plane called a *monoplane*—which had only one set of wings, instead of the usual two sets—was best. The airplane would have only one engine. It would have extra fuel tanks, but it would have nothing on board that was not needed for the flight. That meant no radio to call for help, and no parachute. In order for the airplane to be more streamlined, it would not even have a windshield.

A group of businessmen from St. Louis, Missouri, provided the money Lindbergh needed to have an airplane specially built in San Diego, California. When the plane was ready, Lindbergh named it the *Spirit of St. Louis.*

Lindbergh flew his plane across the country to New York. On the morning of May 20, 1927, he took off from Roosevelt Field, on Long Island, and headed out over the vast Atlantic Ocean. For 33½ hours he fought against the bad weather, the cold, the loneliness, and his growing need for sleep. At last he saw land—the coast of Ireland. He had flown across the Atlantic Ocean!

Lindbergh flew over Ireland, then England, then the coast of France. He landed at Le Bourget Airport, just outside Paris, on Saturday, May 21, at 10:24 P.M.

All during Lindbergh's flight, people in Europe and America had been listening to their radio sets, hoping for news of this brave young pilot. When he landed, thousands of excited people rushed out to the plane and cheered wildly. The news flashed across the world by radio and telegraph—Lindbergh had done it!

Charles A. Lindbergh returned home by ship and was welcomed as a hero. Soon there was a song called "Lucky Lindy" and a new dance called the "Lindy Hop."

Of all the American heroes of the time, Lindbergh was the greatest. And in the 1920's there were many American heroes. George Herman "Babe" Ruth was a sports hero—slugging home runs for the New York Yankees and setting many new baseball records. Fans lovingly called him the "Sultan of Swat" and "the Bambino."

Movies became very popular in the 1920's. One of the most popular movie stars of the time was Rudolph Valentino. He had won fame in a film called *The Sheik.* Many young men slicked back their hair and tried to act like this Hollywood hero.

The 1920's were also good years for American writers. Among the best was F. Scott Fitzgerald, whose stories captured the excitement and glitter of the time. Fitzgerald noticed how popular the kind of music called jazz had become in the 1920's, and named this period of American history "the Jazz Age." Another writer just beginning his career in the 1920's was Ernest Hemingway. He had been wounded in the war and he used his war experiences in several books, including *A Farewell to Arms,* one of his best novels.

It was the business world, however, that made the greatest mark on the era. Many American businesses had grown during the war, and in the 1920's, business boomed. Of all the great business heroes of the Jazz Age, the automobile manufacturer Henry Ford was the greatest. Ford's workers built millions of Model-T automobiles on great assembly lines. The price of a Model-T was so low that almost anyone could afford to buy a car.

Things were not all good in the Jazz Age. In 1920 the United States adopted an amendment to the Constitution that *prohibited,* or made illegal, the making or selling of beer or liquor. Many people thought it was a good thing to outlaw alcoholic drinks, but gangsters soon learned that plenty of Americans still wanted them. The gangsters became rich by selling illegal beer and liquor. They protected themselves with gangs of gun-toting thugs and began taking over and organizing all sorts of illegal activities. This was the beginning of what is called "organized crime."

There were other problems, too. By the end of the 1920's the American business boom was ready to collapse, although few people knew this. For years, people and businesses had been borrowing money and buying on credit, and their debts had been building up steadily.

In October, 1929, people who had used their savings or had borrowed money to buy company stocks and bonds watched as the values of those stocks dropped lower and lower. Many people lost all their money when the stock market "crashed." Banks and businesses began closing, and workers lost their jobs. More and more people had less and less to spend, and this forced even more businesses to close. In a few years, millions of Americans were out of work.

The Jazz Age was over. A new period in American history—the Great Depression—had begun.

The Great Depression
and the New Deal

FOR MOST PEOPLE THE 1920'S would have been a perfect decade had it not been for 1929.

At the beginning of 1929, prices of stocks and bonds soared to new heights. Eager investors bought stocks on the New York Stock Exchange, which is often called "Wall Street" because that is the name of the street where the exchange is located. A few economists warned that the stocks were simply not worth their price tags, but most people paid little heed.

In the fall of 1929 some investors grew uneasy and started selling their stocks. This made other investors panic, and soon everyone was trying to sell their stocks. The stock prices dropped lower and lower.

Banks across the country had invested their customers' money in the stock market. One by one they lost the money they had invested and were forced to close. Nearly 1500 banks closed in 1930.

Factories needed the banks just as much as people did. When the banks started closing, many factories were forced to shut their doors. The workers lost their jobs.

They had no money to buy goods with, and soon many stores were forced to close.

The Great Depression got worse and worse.

Herbert Hoover had been elected President of the United States in 1928. He was an intelligent man and wanted very much to help the unemployed workers. He thought the federal government should help state and local governments set up their own programs to help the unemployed.

Hoover did not want the federal government to interfere with the rights of the state and local governments. Nor did he want it to compete with private business. But he gradually realized that strong action was needed. Congress passed laws establishing new agencies to provide loans to businesses and put people to work on public projects.

But the Great Depression refused to go away. More and more people waited in lines for free food and meals at the "soup kitchens" set up by charitable groups. In every city, homeless people built shacks out of old crates and cardboard. Many accused President Hoover of doing too little to help end the Depression. They called their shack communities "Hoovervilles." People slept on park benches at night, and covered themselves with "Hoover blankets" made up of old newspapers.

A drought struck the Midwest. The hot sun burned out the crops, and thousands of farmers went bankrupt. The banks sold the farms at auction. A sad procession of farm families packed up their few belongings and started west. They hoped to find jobs picking fruit and vegetables in the fertile valleys of California.

People could not understand how American business could go from boom to bust in so short a time. They lost faith in the capitalist system of business that had built the United States. And some began to lose faith in the democratic system of government.

In 1932 Americans prepared to elect a new President. The Republican Party nominated President Hoover for a second term. The Democratic Party nominated the governor of New York, Franklin D. Roosevelt, who pledged "a New Deal for the American people."

Roosevelt knew that ending the Great Depression would take a great effort, but he had faced great problems before. In 1921 he had been struck with polio, a disease that left him unable to use his legs. Roosevelt was a wealthy man, and it would have been easy for him to give up his career in politics and retire to his comfortable home. But Roosevelt was no quitter. He worked harder than ever before. Eleven years later, in 1932, he was elected President of the United States.

As soon as he took the oath of office, President Roosevelt set to work on his plan of action, which he called the New Deal. He got Congress to start new programs and find new ways to put people back to work.

Soon there were many new government agencies to fight the Depression and new laws to help farms and businesses to start operating again.

A new organization called the Works Progress Administration, or WPA, created jobs for more than 2 million workers. WPA workers built many new schools, hospitals, roads, bridges, and parks.

An organization called the Civilian Conservation Corps, or CCC, put young men to work planting trees and rebuilding national parks and forests. The CCC planted more than 200 million trees. Many of the forests we have today were improved by this program.

The Tennessee Valley Authority, or TVA, built dams and power plants on the Tennessee River. It helped farms and factories in a number of Southern states by providing them with inexpensive electrical power and a steady supply of water.

Franklin D. Roosevelt made good use of radio to tell the American people what the New Deal was trying to do. His talks were called "fireside chats." Roosevelt told the millions of families who listened that the only thing they had to fear was fear itself. Americans had to put faith in each other. If they did, they could work their way out of the Great Depression and the United States would be stronger and better than ever.

In 1936 Franklin D. Roosevelt was reelected in a landslide victory. The American people showed they had faith in F.D.R. and the New Deal.

The Great Depression lingered on, but the American people were now united in their effort to fight it and filled with a new hope.

The Second World War—
The Most Terrible War

THE UNITED STATES WAS NOT ALONE in its struggle against the Great Depression of the 1930's. The nations of Europe suffered even greater problems. They had not finished rebuilding from the world war when the Great Depression struck.

Many people in Europe were hungry, homeless, or out of work. Such poverty and unhappiness had helped a man named Benito Mussolini become the ruler of Italy. Mussolini had forced his way into power with an army of black-shirted followers. He declared that he would make Italy into a new Roman Empire, and then all its problems would be over. The people called him *Il Duce,* which means "the leader."

In Germany, an Austrian named Adolf Hitler became the *führer,* or dictator, of Germany. Hitler led a party called the National Socialists, or *Nazis.* He promised great things to the German people. He told them they were better than everyone else, and they should rule the world. Soon Germany was busy rebuilding its army, navy, and air force, and getting ready to make war.

Japan, led by General Hideki Tojo, had already begun a war with China. Tojo and his followers planned to conquer much of Asia and the western part of the Pacific Ocean and set up a "New Order," in which the Japanese would be the rulers. The biggest threat to Japan's plan was the United States, whose Pacific fleet was anchored at Pearl Harbor in Hawaii.

In 1935 Italy attacked the African nation of Ethiopia. Three years later, Hitler's Nazis marched into Austria and made it part of Germany. Then Hitler demanded part of Czechoslovakia. The leaders of Europe were afraid of another war and they agreed to Hitler's demands. Soon Nazi troops marched in and took over all of Czechoslovakia.

In 1939 Hitler threatened to make war on Poland. France and Great Britain warned that they would come to Poland's defense. Hitler thought they would fail to help Poland, just as they had failed to help Czechoslovakia. On September 1, 1939, Germany attacked Poland. Two days later England and France declared war on Germany. The Second World War had begun in Europe.

The United States tried to stay out of the war, just as it had tried to stay out of the First World War. Germany quickly defeated Belgium, Denmark, Holland, France, and Norway. The German *Luftwaffe,* or air force, began bombing Great Britain, hoping it would surrender, too. The British, led by Winston Churchill, were almost beaten, but they refused to surrender.

Germany, Italy, and Japan formed an alliance and called themselves the Axis Powers. It looked as if they might succeed in winning the Second World War.

Then Hitler made a great blunder. In the summer of 1941 he decided to attack Russia. At first the German armies were very successful, but they were stopped in their tracks by the bitterly cold Russian winter. Then the Russians attacked the Germans. What was supposed to be a quick war turned into a long, bloody struggle.

Americans wanted the Axis defeated, but they did not want United States troops to go to war again. President

Franklin D. Roosevelt tried to help the British by making it easy for them to buy food, ships, planes, and supplies.

The United States also tried to get Japan to stop its attack on China by refusing to sell oil and other important supplies to Japan. The Japanese did not like the way the United States was interfering with their plans. They decided to wipe out the whole United States fleet in the Pacific in a single stroke. They sent a fleet of aircraft carriers toward Pearl Harbor.

On Sunday morning, December 7, 1941, Japanese bombers swooped down on the United States fleet at Pearl Harbor. Within hours the fleet was destroyed. More than 80 ships were sunk or badly damaged, including seven of the fleet's eight great battleships. Hundreds of American airplanes had been destroyed on the airfields before they could get off the ground. Thousands of American soldiers and sailors had been killed.

The next day, President Roosevelt asked Congress to declare war on Japan. Soon Germany and Italy declared war on the United States.

The United States had joined the Allies, fighting the most terrible war in history.

At first the Japanese enjoyed victory after victory. But slowly the American and other Allied troops began to win important battles. The Japanese were forced to retreat from the lands they had conquered. Then the United States started bombing Japan itself.

In Europe, United States troops were sent to fight against the Germans and Italians in North Africa. Then American troops invaded Italy. In 1944 the Allies, commanded by General Dwight D. Eisenhower, landed on the beaches of Normandy, France, and began pushing the Germans back to Germany.

As the Allied troops advanced, they came upon vast prison camps, called *concentration camps,* that had been used by the Nazis to murder people. Millions of Jews were killed in the concentration camps. Millions of other people died in the camps as well, but people of the Jewish faith had been the special targets of Nazi hatred and cruelty. The Nazi slaughter of these people during the war has come to be called the *Holocaust.*

In April of 1945, the Italian people rose up against Mussolini and killed him. Soon after, Hitler killed himself. He dared not surrender and answer for his crimes. On May 7 Germany surrendered, and the war in Europe was over.

President Roosevelt had worked very hard to defeat Hitler and the Nazis, but he did not live to see the day of victory. Worn out by years of labor, he had died while on vacation in Warm Springs, Georgia.

It was up to the new President, Harry S. Truman, to force Japan to surrender. Truman's advisers told him that the United States had a new weapon—the atomic bomb. A single airplane with one such bomb could destroy a whole city. The atomic bomb was the most terrible weapon ever invented.

Truman wanted the war with Japan to be over as quickly as possible. He thought that once the Japanese saw what this dreadful new weapon could do, they would surrender immediately and the killing would stop.

On August 6, 1945, an atomic bomb was dropped on the Japanese city of Hiroshima. The city was destroyed, but the Japanese still did not surrender.

Three days later, another atomic bomb destroyed the Japanese city of Nagasaki. At last, the Japanese decided they had had enough of war.

On September 2, 1945, General Douglas MacArthur accepted the surrender of the Japanese aboard the battle-ship *Missouri,* in Tokyo Bay. The world's most terrible war was over.

The United Nations
and World Peace

IN AUGUST OF 1941, when half the world was at war, two great leaders met to discuss how the world could be made a place of peace. The leaders were Winston Churchill, prime minister of Great Britain, and Franklin D. Roosevelt, President of the United States. They met aboard the British battleship *Prince of Wales,* which was anchored off the coast of Newfoundland.

At the end of their talks, Churchill and Roosevelt issued a document called the Atlantic Charter. It stated that the United States and Great Britain hoped to make the world a more peaceful and prosperous place once Germany and the other Axis powers were defeated. They wanted the nations of the world to work together to end war, hunger, disease, and poverty.

The next year, 26 countries fighting against the Axis signed a declaration that called for greater cooperation between nations in working for world peace, prosperity, and human rights. These countries called themselves the United Nations.

In 1945, just as the war in Europe was ending, delegates from 50 countries gathered in San Francisco, California, to create a new organization for world peace.

They called it the United Nations, or the UN for short. The UN Charter, containing the rules by which this new organization would operate, was signed on June 26, 1945. It went into effect on October 24, which we celebrate each year as United Nations Day.

Just as the United States government and many other governments have several divisions or branches, the UN was organized with several branches. The main branch is the *General Assembly,* which has one voting member from each country. The General Assembly votes on important issues brought before it by member nations.

The General Assembly meets during a portion of each year. If some crisis should occur in the world while the General Assembly is not in session, it can be called back into session by the secretary-general, the most important official of the UN. The secretary-general is in charge of the Secretariat, which oversees the different branches of the UN.

The secretary-general has another important job, and that is to bring serious international problems to the attention of another important part of the UN—the *Security Council.*

The Security Council is in session year round. It has 15 members. Five members—delegates from the United States, Great Britain, France, the Soviet Union, and China—are permanent. The other ten members are elected to two-year terms by the General Assembly. The Security Council was designed to be the keeper of world peace. It tries to find peaceful solutions to disputes between nations.

The main purposes of the UN are to keep peace throughout the world, develop friendly relations between nations based on equal rights for each nation, improve living conditions all over the world, and provide a place where nations may meet together.

The first problem facing the UN was finding a place to set up its world headquarters. John D. Rockefeller, one of the world's richest men, gave $8.5 million to the UN to buy land along the East River in New York City.

When the cornerstone of the world headquarters was set into place, the President of the United States, Harry S. Truman, said, "A part of the United States belongs henceforth to the world."

UN headquarters in New York City were completed in 1952. The United Nations also has offices in Geneva, Switzerland, and in Vienna, Austria. The United Nations even issues its own postage stamps, which can be used to send mail from the UN offices to anywhere in the world. UN stamps have been designed by artists in more than 60 countries. They are very popular among stamp collectors.

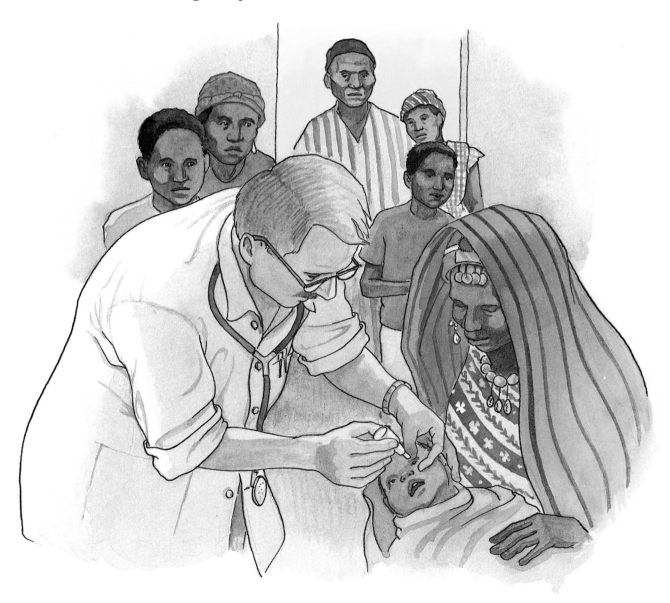

If you visit the UN headquarters, you will see the flags of all the member nations flying in the breeze outside. Nearly a million visitors come to the UN each year. The guides who give tours of the UN come from more than 20 countries. All of them speak English plus at least one other language.

The United Nations has helped to stop fighting in many parts of the world, including the Middle East, Africa, and India and Pakistan. Most of the time, UN forces are concerned with keeping the peace and with seeing that peace agreements are carried out. But in 1950, the United Nations sent troops to defend South Korea from attack by North Korea and China.

The United Nations has worked hard to rid the world of the dangers of nuclear war. It has helped to get international treaties to end nuclear testing in the atmosphere, keep nuclear weapons out of space, and discourage the building of nuclear weapons by countries that do not already have them. There is still much to be done, but the UN has shown the way toward a world free of nuclear weapons.

Most of the UN's efforts go toward helping to improve the lives of people all around the world. Its organizations help the less developed countries produce more food, fight disease, find new sources of energy, create jobs, and give their people a better education. The UN also tries to protect the basic rights of people everywhere—such as life, liberty, equality under the law, freedom of speech, and education.

One of the best-known organizations of the United Nations is UNICEF, the United Nations Children's Fund. Its purpose is to help needy children throughout the world by supplying food, medicine, clothing, and other important items. If you have ever bought UNICEF Christmas cards or helped collect money for UNICEF, you have played an important part in its program.

The Cold War and
the New Frontier

SHORTLY AFTER WORLD WAR II ENDED, the
friendly relations that had grown between the United
States and the Soviet Union during the war began to
disappear. The Soviet Union seemed to be interested
only in gaining control of the countries of Eastern
Europe and in spreading its Communist system throughout the world. The United States wanted all people
around the world to be able to decide for themselves
how to run their countries.

Soon the two great nations were treating each other
like enemies at war—but they did not go to war. So this
period came to be known as the Cold War era.

In 1950 the Cold War threatened to become a hot war
when the Communist government in North Korea sent
its army to conquer South Korea. The United Nations
voted to send troops to stop the North Korean attack,
and President Harry S. Truman ordered United States
troops to go to South Korea to serve in the UN forces.

At first the UN forces came close to defeat, but then
they pushed the North Koreans back. They were close

to defeating North Korea completely when the Communist government in China sent troops to help North Korea.

The war dragged on and on, and no end seemed in sight. In 1952 Americans prepared to elect a new President. Dwight D. Eisenhower, who had commanded the Allied armies in Europe during World War II, was nominated by the Republican Party. He promised to go to Korea and end the war, and in November of 1952 he was elected 34th President of the United States.

Eisenhower served two terms as President. During that time the Cold War continued to trouble the American people. The fighting in Korea stopped in 1953, but meanwhile, the French were fighting a Communist-led uprising in Vietnam, which had been a French colony. A year later they lost a great battle. Vietnam was divided. The Communists took control of North Vietnam. The United States started helping the government of South Vietnam, which opposed the Communists.

In 1957 the Soviet Union became the first nation to launch a satellite into orbit around Earth. A year later, a revolutionary named Fidel Castro came to power in Cuba. Soon he announced that he was a Communist and that the United States was an enemy.

For the most part, however, the eight years of the Eisenhower administration were considered years of progress. The Supreme Court ruled that students could not be put in separate schools according to their race. Such segregation, the Court said, was against their *civil rights*—their rights as American citizens. The country made other advances in civil rights, but progress was slow and often came only after trouble and violence.

In 1960 John F. Kennedy was elected the 35th President of the United States. Kennedy was 43, the youngest man ever elected President. Theodore Roosevelt, who was Vice President under William McKinley, was 42 when he first became President in 1901, but he was not elected. He became President when McKinley was assassinated.

When John F. Kennedy was inaugurated in 1961, he told the American people that a new generation was taking up the task of making the world a better place. He said that the nation was about to open up a New Frontier, and he called upon all Americans to help. He said, "Ask not what your country can do for you—ask what you can do for your country."

Soon young women and men around the country were becoming involved in government and helping to solve the problems facing the United States and the world.

With the New Frontier, President Kennedy hoped to accomplish many important things. During the Eisenhower administration, the United States had launched its first satellite. Now Kennedy wanted the United States to send astronauts to the moon by the end of the 1960's.

A new organization called the Peace Corps was created, and thousands of Americans went to live in less developed countries and help the people there to improve their lives.

New laws were passed to help guarantee civil rights for every American citizen. The federal government also worked to provide better education, health care, and jobs.

But even while he was trying to establish his New Frontier programs, President Kennedy still had to fight the Cold War. In 1961 Cuban fighters opposed to Fidel Castro landed at a place called the Bay of Pigs. They were quickly defeated. Then it was learned that they had been helped by the American government. Although the plan to invade Cuba had begun before Kennedy was elected, he took responsibility for the invasion and its failure.

In 1962 Kennedy learned that the Soviet Union had placed nuclear weapons in Cuba. He demanded that the missiles be removed, and for a time it looked as if the two great powers would go to war. But finally the Soviet Union agreed to remove the missiles.

Kennedy's success in the Cuban missile crisis brought him renewed popularity, but America's role in the growing war in Vietnam was beginning to cause problems.

Like President Eisenhower before him, Kennedy had sent more and more military advisers to help South Vietnam in its war against Communist guerrillas and North Vietnamese troops. Americans were beginning to disagree about U.S. involvement in the Vietnam War.

John F. Kennedy's life came to a sudden and tragic end on November 22, 1963, when he was assassinated in Dallas, Texas. But the hopes and dreams of the New Frontier did not die. The new President, Lyndon B. Johnson, asked the people to continue the work begun by Kennedy. Johnson knew that great problems faced the United States, but he also knew that the American people would find ways to meet every challenge.

The New Explorers: Astronauts in Space

IN MANY WAYS, the story of America has been the story of explorers and exploration. The European explorers of the New World, the early colonists, the pioneers who opened up the American West—all shared a spirit of exploration.

By the beginning of this century, the American West, the last great frontier, was quickly being settled. The nation had grown as much as it could grow. But Americans still had the spirit of exploration. The unknown— the beyond—still beckoned.

In the 1950's, scientists and others around the world looked to space as the last great frontier. The United States and the Soviet Union soon took the lead in what came to be called the "race for space."

In October of 1957 the Soviet Union launched *Sputnik 1,* the world's first artificial satellite. A radio transmitter inside *Sputnik* sent out a steady beep-beep signal as the satellite raced around Earth.

Americans were stunned to think that they had not been the first to put a satellite into orbit. But the Soviets had beaten the United States by only a few months. On

January 31, 1958, America's first unmanned satellite, *Explorer 1,* was sent into orbit around Earth. A few months later, Congress voted to establish the National Aeronautics and Space Agency, or NASA, to run the American space program.

The Space Age had begun.

In October, 1959, a new U.S. space project, called Project Mercury, was started. Its goal was to put a person into orbit around Earth. Seven people were selected to be the first American astronauts. Each of these seven astronauts hoped to become the first human to travel into space. But before that could happen, there were many questions to be answered. Could a person survive in space? What would be the effects of weightlessness? Could a person work in space? Would it be safe for a person to go outside the spacecraft? What type of space suit would be needed?

In 1961 a Soviet cosmonaut named Yuri Gagarin became the first person to orbit Earth. A few weeks after Gagarin made his flight, Alan B. Shepard, Jr., became the first American in space. Shepard did not circle Earth in his flight, but on February 20, 1962, John Glenn became the first American to orbit Earth, aboard his Mercury spacecraft *Friendship 7.*

When John F. Kennedy became President of the United States in 1961, he told the American people that the nation should set a goal of putting a person on the moon by the end of the 1960's. In the years that followed, the United States sent many astronauts into orbit. It also orbited communications satellites to relay radio and television signals, weather satellites to send back pictures of storm systems and cloud formations, and many scientific satellites. The United States also launched space probes to the moon, Venus, and Mars.

By 1969 the United States was ready to send astronauts to the moon. A powerful new rocket had been developed, and the Apollo 11 spacecraft was readied for its mission. Astronauts Neil Armstrong, Edwin "Buzz" Aldrin, and Michael Collins were chosen for the flight.

On July 16, 1969, the giant Saturn V rocket blasted off from Cape Canaveral, Florida, carrying Apollo 11 on its way to the moon. More than 1 million spectators gathered at the Cape Canaveral area to witness the launching. Millions more across the country and around the world saw the launching on television.

Three days later, Apollo 11 went into orbit around the moon. The next day Neil Armstrong and Buzz Aldrin climbed aboard the Apollo 11 lunar excursion module, the *Eagle,* and landed safely on the moon. Michael Collins stayed aboard the main spacecraft, *Columbia,* in orbit around the moon.

Finally it was time for Armstrong and Aldrin to leave the lander and walk on the moon. Armstrong was the first to climb down the ladder of the *Eagle.* As he stepped onto the dusty surface of the moon, his words were radioed back to Earth: "That's one small step for man, one giant leap for mankind."

Shortly after that Aldrin joined Armstrong on the moon. They conducted experiments, set up an American flag, and left a plaque bearing the words, "We came in peace for all mankind."

On July 21 the *Eagle* blasted off from the moon and rejoined the *Columbia,* and the Apollo 11 astronauts began the long trip back to Earth. Three days later, the *Columbia* splashed down in the Pacific Ocean. The mission had been a complete success, and the three happy astronauts were welcomed home as heroes.

American astronauts returned to the moon in November of 1969 and again in 1971. These flights gave scientists important new information about space travel and about the solar system.

Although there were no further moon landings, the space program continued. In 1973 the U.S. launched *Skylab 2,* the first American orbiting space station and scientific laboratory. Two years later, U.S. and Soviet astronauts linked up their spacecraft in the first joint space mission in history, Apollo-Soyuz.

In the 1970's and 1980's the United States launched many space probes to explore the solar system. The probes sent back spectacular pictures as well as vast amounts of new scientific information. In the summer of 1989 the probe *Voyager 2* flew by the planet Neptune and continued on its way out of the solar system. Scientists hope it will continue to send back information for many years.

In 1981 American astronauts flew into space aboard the world's first reusable spacecraft, the space shuttle *Columbia.* Since then, space shuttles have carried many new satellites into Earth orbit and many important scientific experiments have been completed by space shuttle crews.

What lies ahead for the space program? A large, permanently crewed space station, for one thing, and perhaps a permanent base on the moon. It is possible that some day astronauts will even walk on Mars.

The Superpowers
Set the Stage for Peace

THE 1960'S WERE years of great change for the United States. Almost every day there was important news concerning the Cold War, the Space Age, the civil rights movement, new inventions and discoveries, sports, music, and art. And Americans were able to see and hear many of these events through television.

Television had been invented many years earlier, but it did not become popular until after World War II. The first television sets had small screens, and the pictures were in black and white. By the early 1960's, there were millions of color televisions with large screens in American homes.

Television brought to Americans such events as John F. Kennedy's Presidential inauguration in 1961 and the launching into space of Alan Shepard, the first U.S. astronaut in space.

Television captured the scene at Yankee Stadium on October 1, 1961, when Roger Maris hit his record-setting 61st home run of the season.

Television even showed the arrival in New York City of a British rock 'n' roll group called the Beatles; they were making their first U.S. musical tour.

Rock 'n' roll music became very popular in the 1960's. In 1969 some 300,000 young rock music fans went to the Woodstock music and art festival, which was held on a farm in New York State. The people at the three-day event had little food, water, or other necessities, but the festival was remarkably peaceful and successful. Some people even began calling young people of the 1960's the Woodstock generation.

Television also brought unpleasant sights and sounds to American viewers. It showed U.S. troops fighting in a bloody war in South Vietnam. The United States backed the anti-Communist government of South Vietnam, and the Soviet Union supported the Communist government of North Vietnam. The Soviets and the North Vietnamese wanted Vietnam unified under a Communist government.

The U.S. government believed that defending South Vietnam was an important step in the long Cold War against the Communist nations.

At first, most Americans agreed with this policy. But as the years passed and the war grew and grew, many Americans became convinced that the United States should withdraw its troops from Vietnam. Many others believed the United States should do whatever was needed to defeat the Communists. Marches and rallies were held across the nation to protest or support American involvement in the war, and sometimes there were clashes with police. The war in Vietnam caused great unrest and disagreement in the United States.

The last U.S. soldier left Vietnam in 1973. For the first time in many years, no American soldiers were fighting anywhere in the world.

The Cold War continued between the United States and the Soviet Union, but at times it seemed as if the two superpowers were learning how to live together.

In 1972 the United States and the Soviet Union signed a historic nuclear arms treaty. In 1975 the U.S. and the Soviet Union launched a joint space mission called Apollo-Soyuz. Three American astronauts docked their Apollo 18 spacecraft with the Soyuz 19 spacecraft holding a crew of two Soviet cosmonauts. The five space travelers worked and ate together. They held a joint news conference that was broadcast by television around the world.

This new spirit of cooperation ended in 1979, when Soviet troops marched into Afghanistan, a mountainous country located between Iran and Pakistan. Soon the spirit of the Cold War returned to both nations.

In 1980 Ronald Reagan was elected President of the United States. Five years later, Mikhail Gorbachev became the leader of the Soviet Union. At first it seemed as if the two leaders would continue the policies of the Cold War. But people soon began to see stirrings of change in the Soviet Union.

In November of 1985 President Reagan and Mikhail Gorbachev met in Geneva, Switzerland. The two leaders talked alone for hours. When the meeting was over, no major agreements had been reached, but there was a new hope that the two superpowers might eventually work together again.

Mikhail Gorbachev was a practical man and an able politician. He knew that many citizens of his country were unhappy, and that the Soviet system of government needed to be modernized. Backed by like-minded political leaders, he began a program intended to bring a spirit of *glasnost,* or openness, and *perestroika,* or reform, to the Soviet system. He also showed a willingness to negotiate with the United States and other countries to help ease tensions and bring the world closer to real peace.

In December of 1987, Mikhail Gorbachev and President Reagan met in Washington, D.C., to sign a historic agreement. The United States and the Soviet Union both agreed to dismantle all of their nuclear-armed missiles with a range of 300 to 3400 miles. This still left many other kinds of nuclear weapons in the superpowers' arsenals, but the treaty was an important step toward ending the threat of nuclear war.

Soon the Soviet government announced plans to pull all of its troops out of Afghanistan. Gorbachev also announced that some of the Soviet troops stationed in East Germany and other Communist countries in Eastern Europe would be removed. The nations of Eastern Europe, which had been under the strict control of the Soviet Union for many years, began to experiment with reforms of their own.

On New Year's Day of 1989, President Reagan and Mikhail Gorbachev exchanged greetings. In his greeting, Gorbachev said, "Americans seem to be rediscovering the Soviet Union and we are rediscovering America."

Perhaps the two most promising events occurred in Germany in 1990 and in the Soviet Union in 1991.

At the end of World War II, Germany had been divided by the Allies. The eastern part was put under the control of the Soviet Union and soon became a Communist nation; the western part was controlled by Great Britain, France, and the United States and became a democratic nation.

The years that followed in East Germany were marked by the restriction of many basic freedoms. The entire economy was placed under the control of the government, as was most of society.

In 1989 the East Germans began to hold peaceful demonstrations, demanding freedom to travel, vote, and exercise other rights. In November the government announced that anyone who wanted to travel to the West could do so. All the barriers between East and West Germany were gradually taken down and the two countries were reunified into one democratic German state by the end of 1990.

In 1991 Mikhail Gorbachev's leadership role was greatly diminished by a three-day uprising launched by members of the Soviet government. After order was restored, popular support shifted to Boris Yeltsin, the president of the Russian Republic. Yeltsin responded by forging an agreement with the Ukrainian and Belarussian republics to leave the Soviet Union, along with the Russian Republic, and create their own union, called the Commonwealth of Independent States. The establishment of the new union marked the end of the Soviet Union and the end of the Cold War, bringing the dream of world peace one step closer to reality.

What do the coming years have in store for our great nation? Perhaps the countries of the world will finally learn how to settle their disputes without going to war. If that happens, there will be no need for big armies and terrible weapons. Then America will be better able to help solve the great problems of disease, hunger, poverty, and homelessness.